D1586387

Jesus

second
edition

Kevin O'Donnell

Hodder Murray

AN HACHETTE LIVRE UK COMPANY

ACKNOWLEDGEMENTS

The Publishers would like to thank the following for permission to reproduce copyright material:

Photo credits
Cover © Ronald Sheridan/Ancient Art and Architecture Collection Ltd; **p.2** (main image) © Lourens Smak/Alamy, (inset) Michael Ferreira/Rex Features; **p.4** Israel Images/Alamy; **p.5** *tl* Copyright BBC, *bl* © Shai Ginott/Corbis, *br* Robert Fried/Alamy; **p.6** P.RYL.GK.457 Recto. Reproduced by courtesy of the University Librarian and Director, The John Rylands University Library, The University of Manchester; **p.8** Visual Arts Library (London)/Alamy; **p.9** *tl* © ADAGP, Paris and DACS, London 2007; © Private Collection/Photo © Christie's Images/The Bridgeman Art Library, *tr* ©Hamburger Kunsthalle, Hamburg, Germany/The Bridgeman Art Library, *bl* © He Qi, *br* All rights reserved. Vie de Jésus MAFA, 24 rue du Maréchal Joffre, F-78000 VERSAILLES, www.jesusmafa.com; **p.10** *l* © Private Collection/Photo © Christie's Images/The Bridgeman Art Library, *r* © Private Collection/The Bridgeman Art Library; **p.11** *tl* © Alinari Archives/Corbis, *tr* Andrew Holt/Alamy, *br* © Private Collection/The Bridgeman Art Library; **p.14** *l* Rex Features, *r* © Estate of Stanley Spencer/DACS 2007; © Art Gallery of Western Australia, Perth, Australia/The Bridgeman Art Library; p.15 *t* Ilan Rosen/Alamy, *c* Duncan Soar/Alamy, *b* © Peter M. Fisher/Corbis; **p.16** All rights reserved. Vie de Jésus MAFA, 24 rue du Maréchal Joffre, F-78000 VERSAILLES, www.jesusmafa.com; **p.17** Arco/Lux/The Kobal Collection; **p.21** © David Cumming; Eye Ubiquitous/Corbis; **p.22** Robert Fried/Alamy; **p.23** Icon Prod./Marquis Films/The Kobal Collection/Antonello Phillipe; **p.26** © ADAGP, Paris and DACS, London 2007; © Musée National d'Art Moderne, Centre Pompidou, Paris, France/Peter Willi/The Bridgeman Art Library; **p.28** TopFoto/Woodmansterne. By kind permission of The Dean & Chapter of Coventry Cathedral © Coventry Cathedral; **p.29** *t* © Private Collection/The Bridgeman Art Library, *b* © Private Collection/The Bridgeman Art Library; **p.30** *t* © Musee d'Orsay, Paris, France/Lauros/Giraudon/The Bridgeman Art Library, *b* © Antonia Rolls www.antoniarolls.co.uk; **p.31** *tl* Sonia Halliday Photographs (photo by F.H.C. Birch), *bl* David Sanger Photography/Alamy, *r* OSPAAL; **p.32** *t* © Muslim Educational Trust, *b* Joanna Bilska/Alamy; **p.33** © Frans Lanting/Corbis; **p.35** TopFoto/AP; **p.36** Sonia Halliday Photographs (photo by F.H.C. Birch); **p.37** Tretyakov Gallery, Moscow, Russia/The Bridgeman Art Library; **p.38** Austrian National Library Vienna, Picture Archive (Codex 2554); **p.40** *t* © Philippe Lissac/Godong/Corbis, *b* Nolde, Emil, The Last Supper, 1909. SMK Foto/Statens Museum for Kunst, Copenhagen © Nolde Stiftung Seebüll; **p.41** *l* © Pascal Deloche/Godong/Corbis, *r* © Guy Bell/Photofusion; **p.42** *t* Cristian Baitg Reportage/Alamy; *bl* Barry Mason/Alamy, *br* © Basilica di San Marco, Venice, Italy/Cameraphoto Arte Venezia/The Bridgeman Art Library; **p.43** *tl* Mary Evans Picture Library/Alamy, *tr* Crack Palinggi/Reuters/Corbis, *br* ACE STOCK LIMITED/Alamy; **p.44** *t* Jon Arnold Images/Alamy, *b* Eitan Simanor/Alamy; **p.45** *t* © EE Images/HIP/TopFoto, *b* Jonathan Player/Rex Features; **p.46** © P Deliss/Godong/Corbis; **p.49** Courtesy of The Edward Burra Estate, c/o Lefevre, London; **p.50** © Manchester Art Gallery, UK/The Bridgeman Art Library; **p.51** ©newcity/archive; **p.52** ©newcity/archive; **p.53** Courtesy God's Golden Acre www.godsgoldenacre.org.uk; **p.55** *t* © San Francisco, Upper Church, Assisi, Italy/Giraudon/The Bridgeman Art Library, *b* Courtesy Laurie Beth Jones www.lauriebethjones.com; **p.56** *t* © DACS 2007; INTERFOTO Pressebildagentur/Alamy, *b* © British Museum, London, UK/The Bridgeman Art Library; **p.57** 20th Century Fox/The Kobal Collection; **p.58** © Hodder & Stoughton Religious; **p.59** akg-images/ullstein bild; **p.60** *t* By kind permission of Coventry Cathedral © Coventry Cathedral, *b* TopFoto/Woodmanstern. By kind permission of The Dean & Chapter of Coventry Cathedral © Coventry Cathedral.

Text credits
Scriptures quoted from the Good News Bible published by The Bible Societies/HarperCollins Publishers Ltd., UK, © American Bible Society, 1966, 1971, 1976, 1992. **p.13** *F* 'O Come, O Come, Immanuel' translated by John Mason Neale, 1851, *G* 'Born in the Night' by Geoffrey Ainger, reproduced by permission of Stainer & Bell Ltd, London, England, *H* 'Good Christians all rejoice' originally translated by John Mason Neale as 'Good Christian men rejoice', 19th century, *I* 'O Little Town of Bethlehem' by Rector Phillips Brooks, 1868, *J* 'See amid the winter's snow' by Edward Caswall, 19th century; **p.21** *Miracles Do Happen* by Sister Briege McKenna, Veritas Publications, 1998; **p.36** *Mere Christianity* by C S Lewis, HarperCollins, 2001; **p.51** adapted from www.focolare.org.

Every effort has been made to trace all copyright holders, but if any have been inadvertently overlooked the Publishers will be pleased to make the necessary arrangements at the first opportunity.

Although every effort has been made to ensure that website addresses are correct at time of going to press, Hodder Murray cannot be held responsible for the content of any website mentioned in this book. It is sometimes possible to find a relocated web page by typing in the address of the home page for a website in the URL window of your browser.

Hachette's policy is to use papers that are natural, renewable and recyclable products and made from wood grown in sustainable forests. The logging and manufacturing processes are expected to conform to the environmental regulations of the country of origin.

Orders: please contact Bookpoint Ltd, 130 Milton Park, Abingdon, Oxon OX14 4SB.
Telephone: +44 (0)1235 827720. Fax: +44 (0)1235 400454. Lines are open 9.00a.m.–5.00p.m., Monday to Saturday, with a 24-hour message answering service. Visit our website at www.hoddereducation.co.uk

© Kevin O'Donnell 2007

Seeking Religion: Jesus first published 1990

This completely revised edition first published in 2007
by Hodder Murray, an imprint of Hodder Education,
a part of Hachette Livre UK
338 Euston Road
London NW1 3BH

Impression number   5 4 3 2 1
Year   2011 2010 2009 2008 2007

Illustrations by Jon Davis/Linden Artists, Tony Jones/Art Construction, Tony Randell
Typeset in Garamond 11/14pt
Layouts by Lorraine Inglis Design
Printed in Italy

A catalogue record for this title is available from the British Library

ISBN 978 0340 92543 0

Contents

Introduction

What do you know? What do you think?

Most people have heard of Jesus, and most have studied him at some stage in school. This introduction is designed to find out what you know and what you think of Jesus.

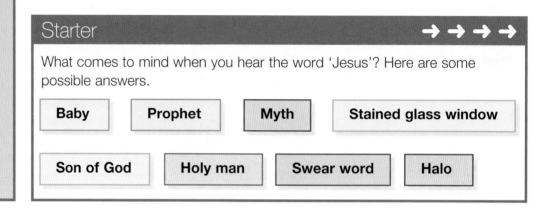

Starter → → → →

What comes to mind when you hear the word 'Jesus'? Here are some possible answers.

| Baby | Prophet | Myth | Stained glass window |

| Son of God | Holy man | Swear word | Halo |

● Jesus spotting

A few years ago a photographer had an idea. He dressed an actor as Jesus and followed him as he walked around London. The photographer secretly filmed the reactions of people.

- Most ignored him. They were embarrassed, maybe, or thought he was a crank to be avoided.
- Some young people knelt down in front of him and said, 'We're not worthy!' Then they ran off, laughing.
- On the Tube, two punk-rockers stopped and talked to him, then hugged him before getting off the train.

▼ We asked our designer to imagine what this situation might have looked like by combining two photos

What do you know?

1 As a class or in groups, spend two minutes recording on a spider chart what you **know** about Jesus. Write as much as you can. These are facts not opinions. If you have written something you are not sure about put a dotted line around it.

What do you think?

2 Read the 'Jesus spotting' text. Explain why each person reacted as they did to the actor dressed as Jesus.

3 What do you **think** of Jesus? Try to sum it up in one sentence.

● A homeless woman who lived on the streets stopped to talk. She told him he looked just like a picture that her mother used to keep beside her bed years ago.

● Walking through a subway, the actor saw another homeless old woman with all her belongings in bags at her feet. As he approached her, she started to swear, picked up her bags and ran away.

It was much the same for the real Jesus. According to the four Gospels (a Gospel is a part of the Christian Bible that tells the story of Jesus), he meets all sorts of people – young and old, men and women, rich and poor. They respond differently. Some invite him home for a meal; some run away in terror; some follow him and worship him; some mock him; some ignore him. Others stop him, talk to him, hug him, ask him for a prayer. One even washes his feet with her tears.

→ → → →   Coming up

This one man, Jesus, has had a huge impact on the history of the world. He founded one of the world's biggest religions – Christianity – although he did not set out to do so. To really understand a religion you have to understand the life, teaching and example of its founders or leaders, so in this book you will examine the life and teachings of Jesus and find out what Christians believe about him.

● In Section 1 you will find out about the **main events** in Jesus' life and the way he affected people around him. You will think about how his life gives people today a sense of meaning and purpose and how his example inspires or challenges them in their faith.

● In Section 2 you will investigate the main beliefs that Christians have about Jesus and how they experience him on their own and together. You will think about the way that people represent these beliefs and experience in **art**.

● In Section 3 you will examine some modern **social and moral issues** and discover what Jesus taught about these and how Christians today try to follow his example.

Throughout this book you will have the opportunity to say what you think of and believe about Jesus.

UNIT 1.1 Real person, real place, real time

Jesus was a real man who lived in a real place at a real time. He was surrounded by real sights, sounds and smells – just as you are. In this unit you find out about the world that Jesus lived in.

Starter

First, start with your world. What sights and sounds surround you?
● Look around the room. What can you see? (Look for tiny things – a speck of paint – as well as big things; far away things as well as things close to you.)
● Shut your eyes. What can you hear? (Listen hard for noises both near and far away.)

1 Choose picture A or C. Imagine you are there. What could you see? What could you hear? What could you smell?

JESUS FILE

Religion: Jewish

Time: First century CE (around 4 BCE–CE 33)

Place: Galilee – a dry, hilly area in northern Palestine, with small villages. Most people worked either as farmers raising animals or as fishermen.

Job: Carpenter or builder.

Language: Aramaic. In Aramaic his name would have been Yeshua Bar Yosif – 'Jesus son of Joseph'.

Rabbi: Jesus could read and write – he was educated. As well as being a carpenter he was a Jewish rabbi – which means teacher.

A

▲ *Galilee today*

YOU NEED TO KNOW ...

■ **Jesus was a Jew** So were his earliest followers.

■ **The Jews believed they had a covenant with God** The Jewish religion was already more than 1000 years old. The Jews believed (and still do) that God has made a special agreement with their ancestor Abraham. This agreement was called a covenant. They believed that God had promised that, if they obeyed him and worshipped him as the only God, then he would bless them (give them land and lots of children and grand-children) and guide them. God gave them rules, or commandments, to follow. These are contained in the first five books of the Hebrew Bible which are known as the Torah, the 'Law' or the 'Way'. All Jewish boys had to learn them or study them.

■ **The Jews were waiting for a Messiah** The Romans had invaded Palestine in 63 BCE. When Jesus lived there it was still an occupied country. The people had to pay taxes to the Roman Empire. Many Jews hoped that God would send a new king of the Jews to set them free, or deliver them. The name of this deliverer was the 'Messiah', or the 'Chosen One'. Some of Jesus' followers believed that Jesus was that Messiah.

B

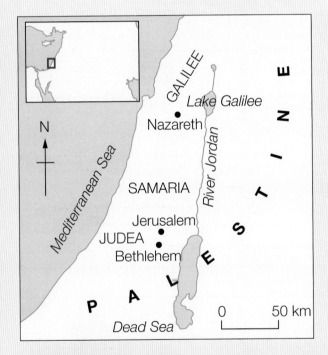

▶ *This is the face of someone of the same race and time as Jesus. He could well have looked something like this*

▲ *A shepherd in Galilee today*

● What did Jesus look like?

The Bible does not say what Jesus looked like and there are no statues of him or paintings from his time. Although we are used to seeing images of Jesus like the one on the cover of this book, these are unlikely to show how he did look.

For a television programme, the BBC tried to discover what Jesus' face might have looked like. They asked some people, who have the skill to build up the shape of a face from the contours of a skull, to work on a skull that had been found. It was of a Jewish man from the first century CE. Picture D shows the result of their work.

The skull did not tell the experts anything about the colour or length of the man's hair, or whether he had a beard, but we know from many other sources that Jewish men of this time – rabbis in particular – kept their hair long and wore beards. Nor does the skull tell us the man's skin colour, but we know that the people of the Eastern Mediterranean are usually dark skinned. As for clothes, we know that Jewish men of that time wore a head covering that fell round their shoulders, a long robe and sandals.

2 Throughout this book you are going to see many different representations of Jesus, such as these.

Flip through the book to see if you can find them. As you work through this book, collect your own copies of images of Jesus from the internet or other books. These will be useful for the summary task at the end of Section 2.

3 Discuss whether or not it matters to you that we don't know for sure what Jesus looked like. Explain your reasons.

Some people wonder if Jesus ever existed. Others think that he did exist but that some of what people say about him has been made up or exaggerated. In this unit you will examine the evidence about Jesus.

Starter

Work with a partner. What do you know about your birth? Write down anything you know. Alongside this write about **how** you know this. For example:

I was born on a Sunday. I know because my Mum told me.

● How were the Gospels written?

The main evidence we have about Jesus is the four Gospels in the Bible. How were they written? Can we trust them?

● EYEWITNESSES

People who met Jesus lived on long after he died. They were able to tell people what they had seen and heard.

● WORD OF MOUTH

In Jesus' time few people could read and write. The way to pass on information was by 'word of mouth' – to tell stories. Today we have computers and cameras to record events, so we may not value word of mouth but in those days most people relied on it and so did it very carefully. In particular, Jewish rabbis trained their pupils to remember and repeat information word for word.

● PIECES OF WRITING

Some of those who could read and write did write down their memories of Jesus. We don't have any of these early accounts but we know they existed. They would have been copied by hand and sent to other people who wanted to find out about Jesus. There might have been hundreds of copies among the followers of Jesus.

● THE FOUR GOSPELS

By the time that the four Gospel writers – Matthew, Mark, Luke and John – sat down to write their stories of Jesus' life, they had three different kinds of evidence to draw on:
- the people still alive who knew Jesus
- the stories that had been passed around
- the pieces of writing.

Historians still debate about the date of each Gospel and the order in which they were written but all agree that they were complete 70 years after Jesus died.

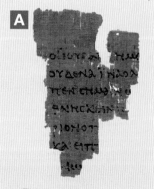

▲ *This is the oldest surviving piece of a Gospel (John). It was found in the desert in Egypt and was copied in about CE 110–130*

● FAITHFUL COPIES

Once a Gospel was written, copies were carefully made by hand. A scribe's job was to make an exact copy, letter for letter. Thousands of these copies have survived. Some have missing pages, others are complete.

What other evidence is there?

Other writers of the time mention Jesus. For example:

- The Roman historian Tacitus wrote about the Christians: 'Christ, from whom their name is derived, was executed at the hands of the procurator, Pontius Pilate, in the reign of Tiberius.'
- The Jewish historian Josephus wrote: 'At this time there was a wise man who was called Jesus … Pilate condemned him to be crucified (killed on a cross).'

However these other writers don't tell us very much else about Jesus.

Why are there four Gospels?

As the Christian church began to grow, the leaders had to decide what to put in the Bible. They chose the Gospels they thought were the most reliable and useful. They chose four written by people who really knew Jesus or who had done the necessary research.

The four Gospels don't agree about everything. Each puts events in a different order and has its own viewpoint and audience. For example, John is very different from the other three; Matthew was clearly written for Jewish readers while Luke was aimed at non-Jewish readers. However, on all of the main facts they agree remarkably – a shared story shines through. Many of the same incidents and sayings are repeated, sometimes word for word, as if they were drawing on information passed on from the time of Jesus himself.

Gospel = good news

The word 'gospel' means 'good news'. The four writers had a message they wanted to share: that Jesus was the Messiah – the Saviour of the world. They wanted people to believe it. From all the things that happened in Jesus' life they selected those that would best make people believe in Jesus.

Gospel = source of authority

A source of authority is someone or something that you take seriously and expect to tell you the truth. Just as in a school a Headteacher is a source of authority, for Christians the Gospels are a source of authority about Jesus, telling them who Jesus was or what he said. They trust the Gospels to tell them the truth about Jesus.

Read more: Luke 1:1–4. Luke starts his Gospel by saying how carefully he has investigated all the previous things that have been said, written and passed on about Jesus.

1 Discuss: Does the fact that there are four Gospels make the evidence about Jesus stronger or weaker? Give reasons.
2 Fill out your own copy of the opinion poll below.
3 Choose one of your answers and write a paragraph giving reasons for your opinion. For example:

I agree strongly that Jesus existed because it is not just the Gospels that mention him. Roman writers say he existed and they would have no reason to make that up.

	Agree strongly	Agree	Not sure	Disagree	Disagree strongly
Jesus existed					
The Gospels can be trusted					
Some of the stories in the Gospels may be made up					
The evidence about Jesus is reliable					

The big picture: the life of Jesus

Before you get stuck into the detail, this unit gives you the overview.

Draw a timeline or 'lifeline' of your life. This can be a straight line or a winding pathway, but you can include only five events.

Jesus' lifeline started in about 4 BCE when King Herod was still alive. The birth stories in the Gospels tell about his birth in the stable, the visit of the shepherds and also of the wise men. Jesus was born in Bethlehem and brought up in Nazareth. The Gospels tell only one story about his childhood – getting lost in Jerusalem when he was 12 years old. When he was about 30 years old, Jesus was baptised in the River Jordan by John the Baptist. Then he began his ministry. He taught, called disciples (chose followers) and healed the sick, mainly around Galilee. After about three years he went to Jerusalem. He was greeted like a king even though he was riding on a donkey. Just a few days later he was arrested, beaten up and then crucified (killed on a cross). Three days later his followers said that they had seen him alive, risen from the dead. His tomb was empty.

1 Pictures A–E show five events in the life of Jesus. Match them to these captions:
- Lost in Jerusalem
- Baptised
- First healing (one of the miracles)
- Crucified
- Born

2 Draw a lifeline for Jesus from 4 BCE to CE 30. Use the text to put the five events in the correct order and then mark them on the lifeline at the correct time.

3 Look at the map on page 5. Where did each of events A–E happen? Read the text for clues.

A

B

C

4 Using a Bible if you need to, add five more events to the lifeline to tell a fuller story of Jesus' life. Give each event a caption.

5 How do you decide which events are important in someone's life? With a partner, write down your standards, or criteria, for deciding whether an event is important.

D

E

Most religions have stories and ceremonies surrounding the birth of its prophet, teacher or leader. Christians celebrate the birth of Jesus at Christmas. This unit looks at what Christians are celebrating.

Starter

What is the best Christmas present you have ever been given? Explain why it was so special. Was it:

- because you had been waiting a long time for it?
- because it was so valuable?
- because of the person who gave it to you?
- for some other reason?

1 Which Gospel tells the story of:
- the shepherds?
- the star?
- the flight to Egypt?

● **The Christmas story and its symbols**

Thanks to Christmas cards, carols and plays, Christmas is probably the most familiar part of the entire story of Jesus. So it may surprise you to know that two of the four Gospel writers don't even mention Jesus' birth at all! What we think of as the Christmas story (called the Nativity – the Birth) is a combination of the stories told by Matthew and Luke. Here are the main points.

---

1 THE ANNUNCIATION

Luke starts with an angel appearing to Mary. He announces that Mary is going to have a child, but not just any child:

A

❛ *The Holy Spirit will come on you, and God's power will rest upon you. For this reason the holy child will be called the Son of God.* ❜

(Luke 1:35)

The news that she was going to have a child would have been shocking enough to Mary. According to the story, Mary was still a virgin. The news that this child would be the Messiah would be even more alarming. However, according to Luke, Mary took it all in her stride.

Read more: Luke 1:38. Read how Mary reacts.

---

2 JOSEPH'S DREAM

Next it is Joseph's turn for a surprise. Matthew describes how Joseph reacted when he found out Mary was pregnant. It was not his child and he feared the scandal that would break out. But an angel appeared to him in a dream and reassured him.

B

Read more: Matthew 1:20–23. Read how the angel convinces Joseph all is well.

3 BIRTH IN A STABLE

According to Luke, around the time Jesus was due to be born, Mary and Joseph had to travel to Bethlehem. So when the baby was born they were away from home and had nowhere to stay.

Read more: Luke 2:6–7. Where do they put the baby?

4 THE SHEPHERDS

Luke next tells the story of shepherds out in their fields. They see a vision of a heavenly choir of angels who sing 'Glory to God in the highest and peace to his people on earth'. The shepherds go to see the baby and worship him.

Read more: Luke 2:19. Read how Mary reacts to the shepherds.

5 THE STAR AND THE WISE MEN

Matthew describes how a star hovers over Bethlehem and guides some wise men, or magi, to Jesus. These magi would have been astronomers, perhaps Jewish, who believed that the star showed that the promised Messiah was about to be born.

We are not told how many wise men there were, just that they brought three gifts. The three gifts were symbolic: **gold** was a symbol of kingship; **incense** was a symbol of divinity (being like God); **myrrh** was a symbol of death (because it was used to preserve, or embalm, dead bodies). Christians see the gifts as symbolising that Jesus was a king, that he was God made man and that he was going to die for humanity.

Astronomers have offered natural explanations of the bright star. Some suggest it was a comet or a supernova (an exploding star), others that it was a conjunction (a joining) of two planets. As stars move closer to each other, for a while they appear as one unusually large and bright star. Such happenings were recorded by astronomers at the time.

Read more: Matthew 2:7–8. Read how King Herod tries to trick the wise men into helping

6 THE FLIGHT TO EGYPT

According to Matthew, Joseph is then warned in a dream that King Herod is going to try to kill Jesus. So he and his family are told to escape to the safety of Egypt until the king dies.

Read more: Matthew 2:16–18. Read what the cruel King Herod did next.

2 The wise men brought symbolic gifts for Jesus (panel 5). What gift would you give to someone really special and why?

3 What symbolic gift would you give to Jesus?

4 We have chosen pictures to illustrate each scene. Use the internet to find a suitable picture for panel 5, or draw your own.

5 Choose one event described on these two pages and explain how this would show a Christian that Jesus' birth was unusual or special.

● Christmas unpacked

Christmas is an important and popular Christian festival. In Christian churches they prepare for it carefully. The month before Christmas is called Advent which means 'coming' or 'arrival'. Some churches have an Advent Wreath which includes four candles, one for each Sunday in Advent.

For Christmas itself churches will be packed full of people. There may be special decorations such as white and yellow flowers, and white and gold banners, and clergy may wear robes of similar colours. There will be a special service with carols and readings from the Bible. Christmas cribs are put on display, recalling the birth in the manger and the coming of the shepherds and wise men.

At these services Christians will be remembering, singing, speaking about, and celebrating two closely related **big ideas**.

● BIG IDEA 1: GOD BECOMES HUMAN

For Christians incarnation is the real point of Christmas. All the other things – the food, the presents, the trees, even the candles and the carols – are unimportant. At Christmas they celebrate God entering the world – his creation – in person, to become human and to live a life on earth. It is like the rich owner of a football club who decides to play himself at centre forward in the first team,

or the writer of a television soap opera who decides to write herself into the plot and appears as one of the characters.

● BIG IDEA 2: JESUS SAVES THE WORLD

God did not come to earth just for fun. Christians believe that God came to earth for a purpose – to save it.

Imagine two miners trapped underground in a mine after an accident, walled up by a rock fall. Rescuers arrive with digging equipment and medicines. Think of the moment they break through that wall to reach the injured miners – they are saved. That is their moment of **salvation**.

The Old Testament prophets had said that a Messiah was going to appear who would bring an end to injustice and suffering, and bring salvation to Israel. The first Christmas was the moment when that rescuer or saviour arrived. Jesus was that Saviour.

F

❝ O Come, O Come, Immanuel, and ransom captive Israel

That mourns in lonely exile here, until the Son of God appear ❞

As well as the two big ideas in the Christmas story, some smaller ideas also inspire Christians today. For example:

- **Obedience to God** Mary was completely willing to do what God wanted. Christians see in this story the importance of being ready to do the will of God, without complaining, however surprising or difficult that may be.
- **Serving the poor** Jesus was born in poverty in a stable, not in a palace as a king. Then his early years were spent in Egypt as a refugee. Christians see in this that they have a special duty to help the poor or powerless.
- **All are welcome** Both wise men and shepherds came to visit Jesus. The wise men were scholars, or possibly even kings, but the shepherds were uneducated and ordinary. Christians see in this that all are welcome at the feet of Jesus, rich or poor, educated or not.

You will come back to these ideas in Sections 2 and 3 and find out how they inspire Christians today as they try to follow Jesus.

G

❝ Hope of the world, Mary's child, you're coming soon to reign

King of the earth, Mary's child, walk in our streets again ❞

Christmas is fun but it is more than that. It is about Jesus, my Saviour, being born. He loved me so much that he came to die for me.

Christmas is colourful and we are humbled to remember that God took flesh and became one of us. He walked on this earth and he felt what we feel. He knows what it is like on the inside.

H

❝ Good Christians all rejoice, with heart and soul and voice

Now we need not fear the grave, Jesus Christ was born to save ❞

▲ Vivien worships in a Christian church in Baghdad, Iraq

▲ Peter worships in a Lutheran church in Stockholm, Sweden

I

❝ O Holy Child of Bethlehem, descend to us we pray

Cast out our sin and enter in, be born in us today ❞

6 Sources F–J come from well known Christmas carols. Work in pairs to summarise what each one says about Jesus.

7 Some people might do all the usual Christmas stuff without ever realising what it really means to Christians. **Either:**
a) Write an announcement, 'The real meaning of Christmas', to be broadcast on all television and radio channels on Christmas morning. You could begin: 'Before you open your presents and cook your turkey, let me explain exactly what this day is about.' You could use the two quotes to help you. **Or:**
b) Design a special Christmas stamp which gets across one key idea about Christmas.

J

❝ Lo within a manger lies He who built the starry skies ❞

8 'Only Christians should be given a holiday at Christmas. Everyone else should carry on working.' In pairs or groups discuss this idea. Is it good or bad? Why?

The Gospels tell us almost nothing about Jesus' childhood and his growing up. The only story is about a visit to Jerusalem with his parents when he was 12. After that the Gospels fast-forward to Jesus aged 30. He is just about to begin his mission of preaching and healing. This unit looks at how he got ready.

Starter

Imagine that you have been chosen to represent the school, your team or your family in some kind of contest. What would you do; whom would you visit; what would you buy to get ready for your challenge?

● The baptism of Jesus

When Jesus was about 30 a man called John the Baptist came out of the desert and preached on the banks of the River Jordan. He was Jesus' cousin and he had spent some time alone, praying in the desert. Dressed in animal skins, he looked wild. He told people to confess their sins to God and to get ready for the Messiah. He told them to wash in the Jordan as a sign that they wanted to cleanse their souls. They were either plunged under the water by him or had it poured over them. This was called 'baptism' from a Greek word meaning 'to be submerged'.

One day, Jesus came to be baptised by John. John was surprised and told him that he was not worthy to baptise him. Jesus insisted. When he went under the water, Jesus had a vision. He heard God's voice saying, 'You are my Son, whom I love; with you I am well pleased.' This was confirmation, to Jesus and to John, that Jesus was the promised Messiah.

● Christ in the wilderness

After he was baptised by John, Jesus spent 40 days fasting (going without food), praying and meditating in the wilderness area outside Jerusalem. John had done the same. Now Jesus was getting himself ready for his mission.

The Gospels say that while Jesus was in the desert the Devil, or Satan, appeared to him and tested him three times by tempting him to use his God-given power.

A

▲ *The baptism of Christ in the film* Jesus of Nazareth

B

▶ Christ in the Wilderness *by Stanley Spencer*

1 Read Mark 1:4–13 for the description of John the Baptist. Design an advertisement to be put up in Jerusalem attracting people to the Jordan to be baptised by John. What will you emphasise: how he dresses, what he does, what he says, or what this all means?

Temptation 1 TO TURN STONES INTO BREAD

Jesus was hungry. But he refused to give in and to abuse his power. His reply came from the Book of Deuteronomy in the Hebrew Bible: 'Man does not live on bread alone, but on every word that comes from the mouth of God.'

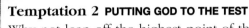

Temptation 2 PUTTING GOD TO THE TEST

Why not leap off the highest point of the Temple in Jerusalem, in public view, and be saved by God's angels? The Devil quoted again from the Bible: 'He will command his angels concerning you, and they will lift you up in their hands, so that you will not strike your foot against a stone.' The temptation was also to show the public his powers and so make people believe. Jesus answered from Deuteronomy again: 'It is also written, "Do not put the Lord your God to the test".'

Temptation 3 RICHES AND POWER

The Devil offered Jesus all the wealth and kingdoms of the world if Jesus were to worship Satan rather than God. Jesus replied: 'Away from me Satan! For it is written: "Worship the Lord your God, and serve him only."' This again is from Deuteronomy. Some people wonder if Jesus had just been reading and meditating upon that text when the Devil appeared.

To Jesus it was something to rely on, a source of authority telling him what was right or wrong.

2 Jesus did three things to prepare for his mission: he was baptised, he fasted and he prayed. For each, explain how this would help prepare him for the challenges ahead. Compare your own preparations you described for your starter (page 14). Why are they similar to or different from those of Jesus?

3 Everyone faces temptations just as Jesus did. Either discuss in pairs or write in a private diary some occasion when you faced and resisted temptation. How did you do it? Were your methods similar to or different from those of Jesus?

UNIT 1.6 The disciples

As soon as Jesus started preaching and teaching around Galilee people were interested. Crowds followed him wherever he went. But he chose twelve people to be his most trusted disciples to share his mission. See what you think of his team.

Starter

Think up a mission to do something special to help someone or to change the world. List your ideal helpers (at least three and no more than twelve) and say why you have chosen them.

● Twelve disciples

The word 'disciple' means a follower or a learner. Scholars think that Jesus chose twelve to represent the twelve tribes of Israel. As well as the twelve there were other people who followed and helped Jesus including a number of women. The twelve were quite an assortment. For example, Simon the Zealot was probably a member of the party of the Zealots, a group of Jews who were violently opposed to the Roman occupation. Here are two of the others.

● SIMON PETER

Simon Peter was a fisherman from Galilee. Luke's Gospel describes how Jesus first called, or chose, him. Jesus wanted to go out onto the lake in a boat to preach to the crowds that were along the water's edge. He asked Simon Peter if he could row him out. After Jesus finished speaking, he asked Simon Peter to row into deeper waters to catch some fish. The fisherman was frustrated and tired after having fished all night with no success but he obeyed. His nets caught a huge shoal of fish. Jesus seemed to have directed him straight to the fish. Simon was amazed and afraid. He knew that he was in the presence of someone very holy. His response was, 'Go away from me Lord; I am a sinful man!' Jesus told him, 'Don't be afraid; from now on you will be catching people.'

▼ The Miraculous Draught of Fishes, *a painting by an anonymous artist*

1 Read about the call, denial and forgiveness of Simon Peter in Luke 5:1–11; Mark 14:66–72; John 21:1–17. Work out a profile of this man and present it to the class.

● MATTHEW

Matthew worked as a tax collector for the Romans. Such people were often hated by their fellow Jews. They worked for the enemy and they often cheated the people. For Jesus to choose a tax collector to be a disciple would have caused a scandal. Matthew followed him straight away. Perhaps he had been feeling guilty and sad that he was working for the Romans, and he felt terrible about himself. Jesus offered forgiveness and a new start, so Matthew jumped at the chance.

2 Work in groups of four. Each look up one of these: Luke 9:1–6; Luke 5:6–11; Matthew 9:9; Matthew 16:15–19. Find out which disciple(s) are being described and what they are doing. Summarise your findings on a large chart.

3 Some people like being part of a team, others don't.
a) Work with a partner to draw up two lists: good things about being in a team; bad things about being in a team.
b) Write a paragraph to explain whether you like or dislike being part of a team and why.

4 Pictures A and B come from different times and different media. Which do you think best shows the relationship of Jesus to his disciples? Write some sentences to explain your choice.

▲ *Jesus with some of his disciples as shown in the film,* The Gospel According to St Matthew

● Ordinary people – extraordinary job

In the Gospels these twelve disciples often get things wrong. They send people away whom Jesus really wants to meet; they misunderstand what Jesus wants them to do; they try to copy Jesus and it doesn't work; they argue among themselves about who is the greatest; when he explains things to them they get the wrong end of the stick.

Even worse, Judas turns traitor and helps the authorities to arrest Jesus. Then Peter – Jesus' first and most trusted disciple, whom Jesus called the 'rock on which he would build his church' – denies he even knows Jesus when someone quizzes him in Jerusalem. And Thomas, later known as the Doubter, refuses to believe.

So this was hardly an 'A team' of brave, skilled heroes. Yet these were the people whom Jesus chose to help in his mission and to continue his work after he died. Their stories reveal the patience and mercy of Jesus as he worked with and influenced people.

The disciples called Jesus 'teacher'. Teaching was the main thing that Jesus did. What did he teach and how did he do it?

Starter

Who was your best teacher at your previous school? Make a list of the things that made him or her a good teacher.

● 'OUR FATHER'

Jesus called God 'Abba'. This is the Aramaic word for 'Dad' or 'Dear Father'. Even though God is a mystery, vaster than the universe and bigger than our minds can understand, Jesus is saying we still have the right to speak to God like a parent.

● The Lord's Prayer

Jewish teachers often gave their disciples a special prayer that summed up their teaching. Jesus did the same. He taught his disciples this prayer and Christians still use it today. This is Matthew's version (Matthew 6:9–13).

Our Father in heaven
May your holy name be honoured
May your kingdom come
May your will be done on earth as it is in heaven
Give us today the food we need
Forgive us the wrongs we have done
As we forgive the wrongs that others have done to us
Do not bring us to hard testing
But keep us safe from the Evil One

● 'YOUR KINGDOM COME'

'The kingdom of God' is not a place. It's more like an attitude. In the kingdom of God people would be ruled by God. And they would be glad to do what God wants instead of following their own ideas.

● 'FORGIVE'

Forgiveness is not soft or easy. It is not saying that something that someone did to you does not matter. It hurt and it was wrong, but when you forgive someone, you let them

off and let go of your anger. You delete it forever and so you give them a second chance, a new start with you.

Jesus lived out this teaching to the very end. As he was dying – nailed to a cross by his enemies – he said, 'Forgive them, Father! They don't know what they are doing' (Luke 23:34).

● 'THE EVIL ONE'

According to the Bible, the world and the people in it are in a battle between good and evil. In the Bible evil is sometimes pictured as a person – the Devil, or Satan – who tempts

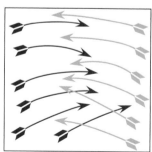

people to abandon or disobey God. God represents good. God is loving and wants the best for people who obey and follow his commandments.

The Gospels show Jesus caught in the middle of this battle – most dramatically when he was tempted in the desert (see page 15). They also show ordinary people caught up in this battle.

Parables

A parable seems to be a simple story but it has a hidden meaning. Jesus often used parables to teach. Sometimes their meaning was very clear but often they were mystifying. His hearers wondered what he meant, but they remembered the stories and discussed them.

There once was a man who had two sons ... (Luke 15:11–32)

The kingdom of heaven is like ... treasure hidden in a field ... (Matthew 13:44)

Suppose one of you had a hundred sheep and loses one of them ... (Luke 15:4–7)

Anyone who hears these words of mine and obeys them is like a wise man who built his house on rock ... (Matthew 7:24–29)

1 Rewrite the Lord's Prayer using up-to-date language or make it a rap.
2 Design a collage to represent one or all of the main teaching points in the Lord's Prayer:
   - Father
   - Kingdom
   - Forgiveness
   - The battle between good and evil.
3 Read the rest of one of the parables in the word bubbles above. Try to summarise its message in no more than ten words.
4 Think of someone whom you would like to be able to forgive, or something that you would like to be forgiven for. Write the name/action on a piece of paper in washable ink. Place the paper in a bucket that your teacher will provide, then watch the water washing away the words. As that happens, imagine yourself letting go of any anger or pain.

→ → → → Coming up

Jesus spent three years teaching and preaching so we can't sum it all up in two pages. But in the rest of this book you will find out more about what Jesus taught and how this inspires and guides Christians in today's world. →

Today we expect doctors to be able to cure almost any illness. But in Jesus' time finding a trained doctor was almost impossible. So when people found out that Jesus could heal people they flocked to him for help. And, according to the Gospels, he did help them. In this unit you will investigate some of Jesus' healing miracles and decide what you think was happening.

Starter

It was long, like a tube, and glowed with a dull light. There were no visible markings or wings. It hovered in the sky. Then it sped off like lightning!

● When you hear a story like this are you a believer or a doubter? Why?
● Talk about some examples of unexplained happenings that you have heard about.

● Ways of healing

There are many ways of healing in our world. For physical healing there are the skills of doctors as well as nature's herbal remedies, healthy lifestyles, exercise and diet. Our emotions need healing too, sometimes as much or even more than our bodies. It is known that bad feelings can make us physically ill as well. For example, a very guilty person might suffer memory loss, withdraw into a form of paralysis or even lose their sight. Emotional healing can come through simple things such as talking to someone and having them listening to us and accepting us.

A

● Jesus the healer

Jesus used different methods of healing too. Sometimes he touched people, laying his hands gently on a person and praying for them. Sometimes he just spoke to them. Once he washed a blind man's eyes with mud and saliva. He healed some people who were far away just by praying for them.

Many of the people healed by Jesus were on the fringes of society. Other people ignored or mocked such outcasts. Jesus behaved differently. He showed love, or compassion. This alone could have had an emotional healing power, but the Gospels suggest that far more than this was happening. Christians believe that Jesus used the supernatural power of God, a power that could speed up healing processes or suspend the normal laws of nature. Here are two examples.

1 Read Mark 2:1–12. What did Jesus say to the paralysed man before he was healed? Why do you think he said it?

● THROUGH THE ROOF (MARK 2:1–12)

A paralysed man was brought to Jesus by four friends. Jesus was teaching in a friend's house and crowds had gathered in the doorway. The friends were unable to get through with the stretcher and so they climbed up the outside stairs onto the flat roof of the house. They made a hole and lowered the man through the roof. Jesus looked at him, said that his sins were forgiven then healed him. The man got to his feet, rolled up the stretcher and walked away.

▲ Leprosy still affects many people today. This man lives in Calcutta. Leprosy deadens the nerves. Because the sufferers can feel no pain in their limbs, they may cut them and get infections. They lose fingers and toes.

● UNCLEAN! (LUKE 17:11–19)

In Jesus' day people avoided lepers. They feared catching the disease. Lepers had to live apart from other people and beg for a living. If lepers were cured, they had to show themselves to a priest to be declared well before they could take their place in society again.

Jesus did not avoid lepers. He spoke to them; he touched them; he prayed for them. Once, ten lepers came to Jesus and asked him to cure them. He declared them healed and they left, cured.

● AUTHORITY

Again and again, the Gospels record that people were amazed that Jesus acted and spoke with authority when teaching and healing. They mean he did so as if he knew exactly what he was talking about and had the right to act. See Luke 4:32, for example.

● **Healing today**

Sister Briege McKenna is a Catholic religious sister. As a young woman she was in a wheelchair, in great pain and taking large amounts of medication for arthritis. Told there was no hope of a cure, she went to live in a convent in Florida where the climate would help her condition. There she went to a retreat, where prayers for healing were taking place. In her book, *Miracles Do Happen*, she describes what happened.

❛I remember looking at the clock as I closed my eyes. It was 9.15 a.m., 9 December 1970. The only prayer I said was 'Jesus, please help me.' At that moment, I felt a hand touch my head and thought it was the priest who had come over to me. I opened my eyes and no one was there, but there was a power going through my body. It's difficult to describe the feeling, but I often describe it this way: I felt like a banana being peeled.

I looked down. My fingers had been stiff, but not deformed like my feet. There had been sores on my elbows. I looked at myself. My fingers were limber (supple), the sores were gone, and I could see that my feet, in sandals, were no longer deformed.

I jumped up, screaming, 'Jesus! You're right here!'❜

Sister Briege felt called to pray for others. Now she travels the world, praying for people to be healed and spreading her message that Jesus can miraculously heal people today.

● **Compassion today**

The healing miracles were nearly always to help the poor. Many Christians today are inspired by Jesus' compassion for the poor and the outcasts. They may not be called, like Sister Briege, to heal such people but they do give practical help, which can bring other sorts of healing to people. Christians believe that Jesus wants his followers to help the poor to improve their situation. You will see examples of charity work in Section 3.

2 Write an imaginary interview with someone who was healed by Jesus. What questions would you like to ask? What answers would you expect?

3 'Jesus was a miraculous healer; Christians model their lives on Jesus; therefore all Christians should do healing miracles.' Is this argument right or wrong? Write a paragraph explaining your view.

Jesus' teaching and healing earned him many friends and some powerful enemies. This all came to a climax in Jerusalem. Each of the Gospel writers describes the final week of Jesus' life in great detail.

1 Look through this story to find all the references to Simon Peter or the disciples. Plot a graph to show Peter's ups and downs through the events described on these two pages. Think about what were the highest highs and the lowest lows. Write a label for each.

Starter

Describe either the worst or the best week in your life. What made it so bad or so good?

● SUNDAY AND AFTER

Into Jerusalem

Jesus rode into Jerusalem on a donkey, along with his disciples. People laid palm branches before him and praised him.

Cleansing the temple

Jesus went to the temple. He overturned the tables of money-changers and tradesmen who were charging people too much. He told them they had made the House of God into a 'den of thieves'. For the next few days he taught in and around the Temple.

Today this is remembered as Palm Sunday. Christians carry palm crosses into churches.

● THURSDAY **Last Supper**

Jesus and his disciples shared the traditional Passover meal together in Jerusalem. At the meal Jesus washed the disciples' feet. He prayed for them. He told them he was going to die. He told them one of them was going to betray him. Jesus offered bread and wine to his disciples to eat and drink, saying that these were his body and his blood. He told them to keep doing this even after he had left them.

Christians continue to do this, some every Sunday. Once a year on Maundy Thursday, as it is now called, leaders are supposed to become servants and wash poor people's feet.

The arrest

Later, as his disciples slept, Jesus prayed for hours in a garden outside Jerusalem. Temple guards and Roman soldiers came to arrest him. Judas, one of his own disciples, showed them where to find him.

In some churches today Christians have hours of prayer to remember this time.

Peter's denial

Simon Peter went to the High Priest's house where Jesus was being tortured. As Simon waited in the courtyard, warming himself by a fire, some people recognised him as a disciple. Three times Peter denied that he knew Jesus, then a cock crowed. This is what Jesus had foretold. Peter was deeply ashamed.

● FRIDAY **On trial**

Jesus was brought before Pontius Pilate, the Roman governor, accused of being a troublemaker and of claiming to be a messiah or king. Pilate was reluctant to condemn an innocent man, but he finally sentenced him to be crucified (killed on a cross).

Journey to the cross

Jesus was given his own cross to carry. As he walked through Jerusalem he was mocked by some and helped by others.

> In many Catholic churches this journey is commemorated with a set of pictures called the Stations of the Cross. Worshippers pray before each one, remembering the suffering of Jesus.

Jesus dies

Jesus was nailed to a cross. Two thieves were crucified too. One repented his sins and asked for Jesus' help. The other mocked Jesus. Jesus died around 3.00 pm. According to Matthew, there was a violent storm and earthquake when he died.

> Christians hold a special service to remember Jesus dying on that day – 'Good Friday'. Some honour Jesus by touching or kissing a cross.

The tomb

Jesus' body was taken to a tomb, cut into a hillside, in the garden of one of his secret followers, Joseph of Arimathea. The entrance was sealed with a huge stone.

● SUNDAY The Resurrection

Jewish people do no work on the Sabbath (Saturday) so it was two days later, early on Sunday morning, that some of Jesus' female followers went to the garden tomb to prepare Jesus' body properly for burial. But they found that the stone at the entrance was rolled aside and the tomb was empty. An angel told the women that Jesus had risen from the dead.

> Christians hold special services on Easter Sunday to celebrate the Resurrection. The day is regarded as the beginning of the Church year.

The first appearance

One of the women saw Jesus but mistook him for the gardener. Jesus told her that he was alive and that she should go and tell the rest of the disciples what had happened. The women hurried away.

● SOME DAYS LATER More appearances

The disciples had locked themselves inside an upstairs room in Jerusalem. They were afraid of being arrested. At first they did not believe the women's story that they had seen Jesus but then they too met Jesus many times over the next few days. Jesus blessed his disciples and encouraged them to have faith. He could be touched, but he could also walk through walls or locked doors and could move from place to place instantly.

Peter forgiven

Simon Peter in particular had unfinished business with Jesus. When Jesus met Peter by the lakeside he asked Peter three times: 'Do you love me?' Peter's denial of Jesus was forgiven and forgotten. Jesus told Peter to 'feed his sheep' (to look after his followers).

● SOME WEEKS LATER The Great Commission

At the end of the Gospels, the risen Jesus appears one last time to his disciples on a mountain. He tells them they must continue the work he was given to do (Matthew 28:18). Some see this as the moment that the Christian church was born.

2 Christians call this Holy Week. Churches have rituals and services – the main ones are in a box – to mark each event and to inspire and challenge people in their faith. Choose one of the events and try to find out more about it. If you can, interview someone to ask what this service or ritual means to them – how it inspires or challenges them.

Did Jesus really rise from the dead?

The Gospel writers were in no doubt: after Jesus was crucified he came back to life. They say he was seen and heard by hundreds of people.

Not everyone is so easily convinced. They have other explanations for the empty tomb and the appearances of the 'risen Jesus'. But there are problems with the other explanations too.

I think that the disciples stole the dead body then made up the story of the Resurrection.

Remember that the tomb was guarded by a group of armed Roman soldiers and sealed with a heavy stone.

I am sure they could have moved the stone.

The disciples stuck with their story through awful persecution. Their faith never wore off. Even when threatened with death they did not give up their belief that Jesus had risen from the dead. Would they have done that for a lie?

Well, maybe the Jewish or Roman authorities stole the dead body.

But why would they do that?

Because they did not want any of Jesus' followers stealing it and pretending he had risen.

But they were against Jesus. If they had the body, all they had to do was show it to everyone and the whole Resurrection story would be exposed as a myth. They would have finished off Christianity for good.

Possibly Jesus did not die – the disciples nursed him back to life. When he had recovered he 'appeared' to people as if he had risen from the dead.

If Jesus had survived crucifixion he would still have been terribly wounded. He would have taken months to recover. Would he really have been able to convince so many people that he had actually risen from the dead?

Maybe they sincerely believed but were deluded. The resurrection appearances were a mass hallucination – wishful thinking.

Hallucinations wear off. This one didn't.

It could have been a metaphorical resurrection – Jesus rose again in the disciples' hearts.

But that isn't what the disciples taught. They said that they really had seen him.

3 Which of these explanations do you believe?
- The disciples stole the dead body.
- The Jewish or Roman authorities stole the dead body.
- Jesus did not really die. The disciples nursed Jesus back to life.
- It was a mass hallucination.
- It was a metaphorical resurrection.
- It was a literal resurrection. What the Gospel writers say is true.

Write a paragraph to explain your choice.

Summary tasks

Choose one of these tasks. The first one is quite hard; the second should be easier.

● Jesus board game

Design a board game about the life of Jesus. It should give players an overview of his life. Here are some tips but you may have your own ideas of how to do it.

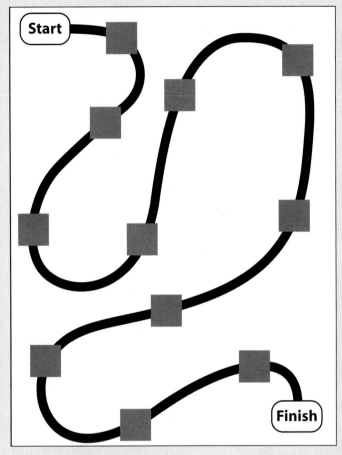

- On a piece of A3 paper, draw a pathway like this that leads from the Annunciation to the Great Commission.
- Choose several events in the life of Jesus. (You could choose events covered in Section 1, such as the calling of the first disciples or the Last Supper, or you could include others that you know about.) In squares on the board, mark as many as you want and make sure they are in order.
- Write a factual question about each event, e.g. 'Who was Jesus' first disciple?' If players land on the square and answer correctly, they earn points – the more the better. Knowing things is important. You could grade your questions – easy, 1 point; average, 2 points; hard, 3 points.
- Use the blank squares in different ways. Some could be Opinion squares. Write some multiple-choice Opinion cards. When players land on these squares, they have to pick a card and state their opinion about Jesus. Having opinions is also important.
- Make some disciple playing pieces like these ones below and stick them on card. Find some dice and start playing!

● TXT GSPL

Write a txt msg about Jesus 2 snd 2 sm1 who hs nvr herd of him. Max 300 wds.

UNIT 2.1 | Images of Jesus

Jesus never intended to found a new religion, yet within a few hundred years of his death Christianity had swept across Europe. It now has more followers around the world than any other religion. In Section 2 you will find out more about how Christians makes sense of Jesus today: what they believe about him; how they worship him; how they express their hopes, sorrows and wonders in art and music and pilgrimage.

Starter

Look at picture A. What impression does this give you of Jesus? Do you agree with the speech bubbles (below left)? Work with a partner to write down your reactions to this picture.

I like the colours.

It doesn't look at all like Jesus.

He looks scared.

▶ Head of Christ, *painted by Georges Rouault, 1910. Rouault trained as a maker of stained glass before he became a painter*

26

There is no such thing as an 'accurate' picture of Jesus. All pictures are interpretations which reflect the attitudes and beliefs of the artist. In this unit you will examine various images of Jesus and investigate the beliefs about Jesus that they express.

There are millions of pictures of Jesus. Artists have been painting him for centuries. In Section 1 alone there were 11. On pages 28–31 you will see some more done at different times, in different media and on different themes. Information, notes and questions are provided to help you interpret them. There is also a checklist opposite for you to follow.

1 Working as a group, divide the pictures among you and analyse your chosen picture.
2 Present your findings to the rest of the group. What does this picture say about Jesus?
3 As a group, choose two pictures which best show these beliefs:
   ● Jesus suffered for human beings
   ● Jesus was God on earth
   ● Jesus was a non-conformist who stirred things up.
   Explain your choices.
4 Now think about opposites. Choose two pictures that belong at different points on these lines.

   God ———————————— Man

   Meek ———————————— Strong

   Explain your choice and the positions.
5 Think of other contrasts of your own and choose two pictures that belong at different points on your line.
6 Choose two images that you think would most appeal to **a)** Christians **b)** non-believers, or atheists. Explain your choices.

→ → → →　　　Coming up

At the end of Section 2 you will be asked to present a Jesus arts exhibition showing how artists have expressed different beliefs about Jesus. As you work through this section, note any images that you strongly like or dislike, or that interest you. →

● How to read a picture of Jesus

Context: Who made it, when, where and why? Look at the caption and notes to help you.

Title: Does this give you a clue to what the artist is interested in?

Jesus:
● **His face** Sad? Happy?
● **His eyes** Looking at you? Looking away?
● **His attitude** Gentle? Authoritative?
● **His race:** What ethnic group does this Jesus come from?
● **His clothes** Jesus is sometimes shown in shining white, sometimes in everyday clothes of his time or ours.

Story/theme: Some pictures are drawn from a Gospel story – a particular moment in Jesus' life. What is the story shown in this picture? How are other characters reacting to him? What aspect of Jesus does it highlight – his miracles, his authority, his teaching, his challenge?

Setting: Some artists put Jesus in a modern day setting. What effect does that have?

Shape, colour and tone: These are the main techniques used by artists to convey mood. How have they used them?

Symbols: Religious pictures are often packed full of symbols – for example a dove, a book, a halo. What symbols do you see?

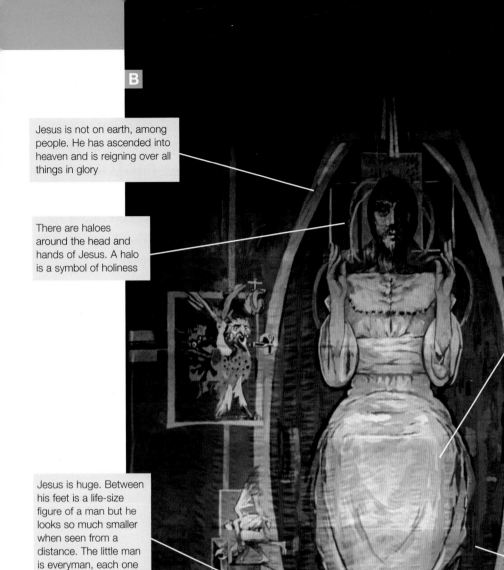

B

Jesus is not on earth, among people. He has ascended into heaven and is reigning over all things in glory

There are haloes around the head and hands of Jesus. A halo is a symbol of holiness

Jesus is huge. Between his feet is a life-size figure of a man but he looks so much smaller when seen from a distance. The little man is everyman, each one of us

The artist has used bright white and patches of gold. Gold is a precious metal and is a symbol of kingship

The four creatures represent the Gospel writers: Matthew – the man; Mark – the eagle; Luke – the ox; John – the lion. Here they represent the good news being sent out to the four corners of the world

Light often symbolise heaven or holiness. The dark spaces contrast with the ligh The dark surrounding the figure of Jesus suggests mystery

▶ Christ in Glory, *a tapestry in Coventry Cathedral by Graham Sutherland, 1962*

Circles suggest eternity for they go round and round forever

◀ Menorah, *painted by Roger Wagner, 1990s. The artist had been working on a painting of Christ's crucifixion. Then one day he was travelling by train past the power station and was so overwhelmed by its scale and power that he put his crucifixion scene in that setting*

In the background is Didcot power station near Oxford

After he had finished the picture, the artist noticed how the six towers and the chimney reminded him of a menorah, a seven-branched candlestick which is a Jewish symbol of God's presence, so he used that title

In the middle ground is the crucifixion of Jesus

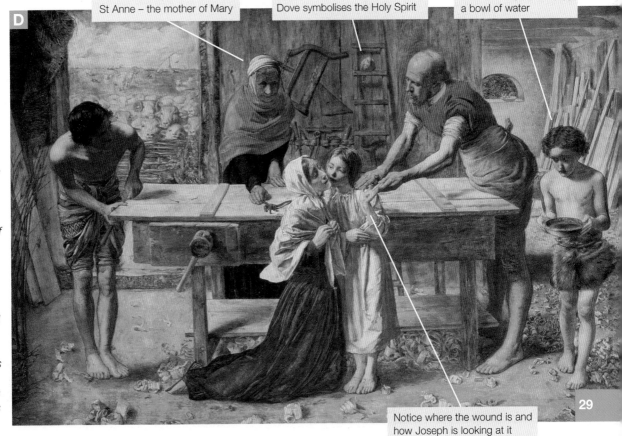

St Anne – the mother of Mary

Dove symbolises the Holy Spirit

John the Baptist carrying a bowl of water

▶ Christ in the House of his Parents, *painted by John Millais, 1849. Millais was one of the most popular and skilled artists of his time. In this picture – painted when he was only 20 – he shows an imagined moment in Jesus' childhood as Jesus is comforted by his mother after he has hurt himself. Millais always included lots of detailed symbols in his paintings*

Notice where the wound is and how Joseph is looking at it

Dinner guests

Why are everyone's eyes focused on Jesus?

What is he doing?

Why is Jesus dressed differently from the rest of the dinner guests?

Which figure do you think is Simon the Pharisee?

Prostitute at Jesus' feet

▲ Christ in the House of Simon the Pharisee, painted by Jean Beraud. Jean Beraud (1849–1935) lived for most of his life in Paris, painting everyday life. Here the setting is nineteenth-century Paris and the dinner guests are respectable, wealthy Parisian businessmen

A posh area of London

Jesus is painted as an Orthodox icon, with a halo and a rich robe

◀ Jesus on the Tube, painted by Antonia Rolls, 1990s. Antonia Rolls first got interested in religious art when she was only five years old. Her father showed her a picture of Jesus being taken down from the cross and she was shocked by it. She said the painting was tragic and quite horrific. She had not seen anything like it before. It was then she realised the power of painting and decided to be an artist

G

...s right hand holds a Gospel

◄ Christ Pantocrator, *painted in Monreale Cathedral, Sicily. Pantocrator means 'ruler of all'. In the Middle Ages the most common image of Jesus was the one shown in this picture. There were thousands of pictures like it around Europe*

As usual around his head is a halo – symbol of holiness – but through it there is a cross – symbol of crucifixion and salvation. This shows that Jesus had to suffer and die for humanity before he could enter the glory of heaven

Jesus' left hand is raised in the pose of a teacher

His clothes are luxurious, almost royal

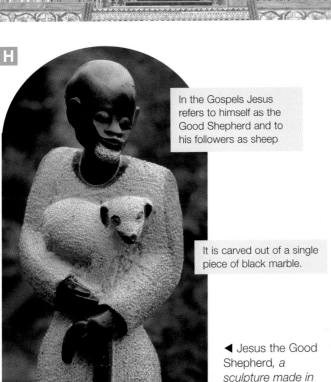

H

In the Gospels Jesus refers to himself as the Good Shepherd and to his followers as sheep

It is carved out of a single piece of black marble.

◄ Jesus the Good Shepherd, *a sculpture made in South Africa*

I

This artist shows Jesus as a freedom fighter.

▲ Jesus with Gun. *In the 1970s some Christians in Central and South America joined in armed revolutions against their governments. They believed that Jesus was on their side because he had promised liberation for the poor. Other Christians in these countries did not rebel but protested peacefully and campaigned for justice. All of them believed that Jesus is on the side of the poor. This way of thinking about his message is called 'liberation theology'*

31

Jesus is respected and honoured by many members of other world religions. They might not believe the same things about him that Christians do but they regard him as an outstandingly holy man, a prophet, a teacher or one of many gods who came to earth.

Starter → → → →

Think of a friend or a famous person who means a great deal to you. How do others see him or her? What do they agree and disagree about?

● Islam

To Muslims, Jesus was the greatest Prophet before Muhammad. They call him Isa. They believe he was born of the Virgin Mary as a miracle to show the power of Allah. They believe he worked miracles and was the Messiah. He was a word sent from Allah. However they do not believe that he was God – Jesus was just a man – or that he died on the cross – it only appeared that he did. They believe that Jesus was taken up to heaven and he will return before the final Judgement.

❝I am the servant of Allah. He has given me the Gospel and ordained me as a prophet. His blessing is upon me wherever I go.❞

(Jesus speaking in the Qur'an, the Muslim holy book)

A

Prophets of Allah

Ādam آدم	*Adam*
Idrīs إدريس	*Enoch*
Nūh نوح	*Noah*
Hūd هود	
Sālih صلح	
Ibrāhīm إبراهيم	*Abraham*
Ismā'īl إسمعيل	*Ishmael*
Ishāq إسحق	*Isaac*
Lūt لوط	*Lot*
Ya'qūb يعقوب	*Jacob*
Yūsuf يوسف	*Joseph*
Shu'aib شعب	
Ayyūb أيوب	*Job*
Mūsā موسى	*Moses*
Hārūn هرون	*Aaron*
Dhul Kifl ذوالكفل	*Ezekiel*
Dāwūd داود	*David*
Sulaimān سليمن	*Solomon*
Ilyās إلياس	*Elias*
Al Yasa' اليسع	*Elisha*
Yūnus يونس	*Jonah*
Zakarīyā زكريا	*Zechariah*
Yahyā يحيى	*John*
Īsā عيسى	*Jesus*
Muhammad محمد	
(peace be upon them)	

▲ The 25 prophets mentioned in the Qur'an

▼ A Buddhist version of Leonardo da Vinci's Last Supper, from Darjeeling, India

B

● Buddhism

Buddhists see Jesus as an enlightened spiritual teacher. Like the Buddha in ancient India, he taught people the Way to peace and life. To Buddhists it is not important whether he was God. What is important is how your beliefs and attitudes help you live your life on this earth.

C

▲ *Jesus and the Hindu god Ganesha featured on a poster*

Hinduism

Hindus believe God has appeared on earth in hundreds of different ways through history. Jesus may be one of those appearances. Hindus will sometimes include a statue of Jesus alongside images of Hindu gods such as Vishnu. Some even pray to Jesus.

The Indian leader Gandhi, who was a Hindu, used to say that he wept as he looked at a picture of Jesus on the cross. In Jesus he saw all innocent people suffering.

Judaism

Jesus was a Jew, as were all the first disciples. Although some Jews today do accept him as the Messiah, the majority do not. They respect Jesus as a great teacher of the Torah, the Law of Moses. They see him as one of the wandering holy men of his time who prayed for the sick and taught the love of God.

Humanism

Humanists reject all religion but they still respect Jesus as a great teacher. Although they may criticise some of the things he said because they think his view of the world is out of date and superstitious (for example, they believe there is no such thing as heaven or hell), they find other things he said acceptable (for example, his moral teaching about forgiving your enemies guides people away from violence).

❝You have heard that it was said, 'Love your friends, hate your enemies.' But now I tell you: love your enemies and pray for those who persecute you.❞

(Matthew 5:43–44)

1 Copy and complete a chart like this about Jesus in different religions. Use ticks or explanations.

Religion	God	A god	A prophet	A teacher
Christianity	Jesus is God in human form			

2 When you have finished, write a sentence to show what they all have in common.

The more you know about Christian beliefs about Jesus, the more you will be able to understand pictures of him. In this unit you will examine some of the main ideas.

Starter → → → →

Have you ever been rescued? If so, tell others what happened. Who rescued you? How did they do it? How did you feel?

● Salvation

Christians call Jesus 'Saviour'. What does this mean?

The world is not all bad and people are not all bad but Christianity teaches that evil is real and that the results of evil in the world are sin, death, war, destruction and failure. These things have been part of human experience ever since the start of time. People need to be saved from these things, now and always. Christians claim that Jesus is God's way of doing this and that everything that happened to Jesus was part of God's plan.

You could spend a lifetime understanding how this happens. Indeed, people have spent 2000 years trying to explain **salvation**. It can get very complicated and not all Christians agree – but here is one way of showing it.

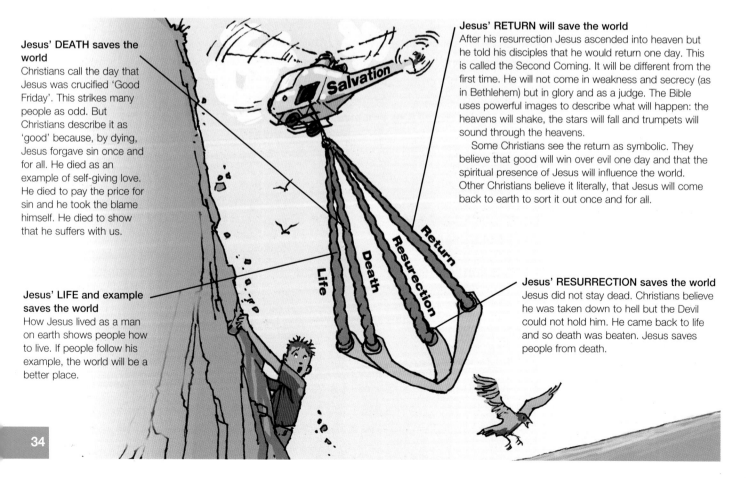

Jesus' DEATH saves the world

Christians call the day that Jesus was crucified 'Good Friday'. This strikes many people as odd. But Christians describe it as 'good' because, by dying, Jesus forgave sin once and for all. He died as an example of self-giving love. He died to pay the price for sin and he took the blame himself. He died to show that he suffers with us.

Jesus' LIFE and example saves the world

How Jesus lived as a man on earth shows people how to live. If people follow his example, the world will be a better place.

Jesus' RETURN will save the world

After his resurrection Jesus ascended into heaven but he told his disciples that he would return one day. This is called the Second Coming. It will be different from the first time. He will not come in weakness and secrecy (as in Bethlehem) but in glory and as a judge. The Bible uses powerful images to describe what will happen: the heavens will shake, the stars will fall and trumpets will sound through the heavens.

Some Christians see the return as symbolic. They believe that good will win over evil one day and that the spiritual presence of Jesus will influence the world. Other Christians believe it literally, that Jesus will come back to earth to sort it out once and for all.

Jesus' RESURRECTION saves the world

Jesus did not stay dead. Christians believe he was taken down to hell but the Devil could not hold him. He came back to life and so death was beaten. Jesus saves people from death.

● Sacrifice

If you chose any of the ropes in the diagram – for example, the 'Death' rope – and unravelled it, you would find it was made of lots of smaller strands like this.

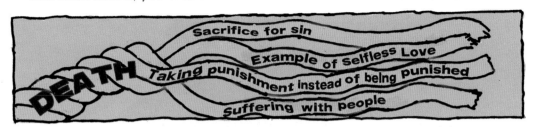

These ideas are all important but we are going to focus on just one. This story should help you understand the idea of sacrifice.

Maximilian Kolbe's sacrifice

Father Maximilian Kolbe was a Polish Catholic priest who was also a Franciscan friar. As a friar he lived by three rules: poverty, obedience and chastity. He was to live simply, serving others, obeying God and remaining single.

During World War II Maximilian was in Poland when Hitler's troops invaded. The friars helped about 3,000 refugees, among them Jews fleeing from the Nazi concentration camps.

After Maximilian published a magazine urging people to speak the truth and to resist Nazi evil, he was sent to Pawiak prison, where he was beaten. Later he was transferred to Auschwitz camp, an extermination camp. People were sent there to be killed immediately or else worked to death. He was given heavy work, moving concrete blocks. Despite the harshness, he wrote, 'the good Lord is everywhere and holds every one of us in his great love.'

One day in 1941, everyone was lined up and counted. Three men had escaped. As punishment, ten other men were chosen to die, by starving to death in the Bunker, an underground cell. One of the ten, a man called Franciszek Gajowniczek, called out, 'O my poor wife! My poor children! I shall never see them again.' At that moment Maximilian stepped forward and asked the guard if he could exchange places with the man. The guard was taken aback but didn't care who died. The exchange took place. Someone who worked in the Bunker wrote later about what happened at the end:

'In the cell of the poor wretches there were daily loud prayers, and singing. Prisoners from neighbouring cells also joined … I had the impression I was in a church. Fr Kolbe was leading and the prisoners responded. They were often so deep in prayer that they did not hear that the inspecting SS men had descended to the Bunker … Fr Kolbe did not beg and did not complain but raised the spirits of the others.'

Maximilian was the last to die. A guard gave him an injection of carbolic acid which killed him. He died with a prayer on his lips.

Maximilian Kolbe was declared a saint on 10 October 1982 by Pope John Paul II. The man whose life he had saved was present. Jesus said, 'The greatest love a person can have for his friends is to give his life for them' (John 15:13). Kolbe had died so that this man might live.

1 Discuss the story of Maximilian Kolbe.
a) Who was saved by Kolbe's sacrifice?
b) Why do you think Kolbe did this?
c) Do you think Kolbe did a brave or a foolish thing and why?
d) How is Kolbe's death like Jesus' death? How is it different?

2 a) Create your own design for an artwork to place in a church to express the idea of salvation. You could use words, colours, shapes, collages or painting.
b) Write a paragraph to explain it.
c) At the end of Section 2 you might wish to include this artwork in your Jesus arts exhibition.

● Was Jesus God?

In the Gospels Jesus himself never says 'I am God' but he is credited with some very startling words and some surprising actions.

● **WORDS**

I am the Bread of Life

I am with you always, to the very end of the age

Whoever has seen me has seen the Father

I am the Resurrection and the Life

I am the Way, the Truth and the Life

'I am' was an ancient title for God in the Hebrew Bible (e.g. Exodus 3:14).

A true record? Some people explain these statements by suggesting that, rather than recording the actual words of Jesus, the Gospel writers put a gloss on what Jesus said. But for Christians who believe that the Gospels tell the truth about Jesus there is no problem in accepting them. They argue that a man who said things like this should be taken very seriously. If not,

❝*A man who was merely a man and said the sort of things Jesus said would not be a great moral teacher. He would either be a lunatic – on a level with a man who says he is a poached egg – or else he would be the Devil of Hell.*❞

(*CS Lewis in* Mere Christianity)

● **ACTIONS**

In the Gospels, Jesus' birth was a miracle – his mother was a virgin – and in his life Jesus was a miracle worker as well as a teacher. Jesus walked on water, fed 5,000 with bread and fish, calmed a storm and finally rose from the dead and ascended into heaven. These are the kinds of things God might be able to do but not an ordinary man, even if he were a wise teacher.

A true record? People have come up with human explanations for some of these miracles. For example, when Jesus fed 5,000 people, maybe some had brought their own food but were selfishly hiding it because they did not want to share. Then, when the little boy brought his loaves and fish to Jesus, everyone else was shamed into sharing and so there was more than enough food. The real miracle was the change in people's hearts.

But for those Christians who believe that Jesus was God such explanations are unnecessary and irrelevant. If Jesus were God he would have the power of God in him, for example, to control the natural world. God 'incarnate' could have suspended the normal laws of physics and controlled the weather.

● **WHAT DO YOU THINK?**

Of course these words and actions can never be proved. They are matters of faith. You either believe them or you don't! According to the Gospels the disciples were quite slow to believe. Even near the end of the Gospels they are only just beginning to grasp what was different and special about Jesus, so if you are doubtful too you are like them. They did come to believe in the end, so firmly that they were prepared to die for their faith.

The Trinity

Christians teach that there are three aspects to God, known as the Trinity:

- God the Father – who created the world and keeps it going
- God the Son (Jesus) – who came to earth and lived a human life
- God the Spirit – who inspires and guides Christians from day to day.

3 Picture A is one artist's attempt to show the Trinity. The artist does not think that this is what the Father, Son or Spirit looks like. He is trying to convey the idea of 'three in one' through symbols. Do you think you could do better than Rublev in showing the idea of the Trinity? How would you try to show how three things can be one at the same time?

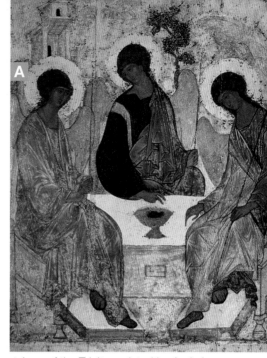

A

▲ Icon of the Trinity, *painted by Andrei Rublev, 1400s*

Prophet, teacher or God?

If Jesus were a prophet he would be ... a messenger from God. He would still be a human being, not an angel or anything like that. A prophet is not God himself but a person who is given some understanding or message that he could not have got on his own from common sense. This is what most Muslims believe.

If Jesus were a good teacher he would be ... an ordinary human being who could understand people and could use his natural skills to help others understand too. Teachers can become good teachers just by studying a subject and working to improve themselves. They don't need a revelation from God. This is what most Humanists believe.

If Jesus were God he would be ... the creator of the universe come down to live on earth as a human being. He would not be a normal human being – he would have God-like qualities, such as the ability to do miracles, to calm storms, to heal people, to come back to life after he died – but he would still have human qualities too. This is what Christians believe.

4 You are going to write a speech for a debate. You can argue that Jesus was a prophet or was a good teacher or was God (or use another viewpoint if you know one). Your speech should show that you have considered other points of view and should explain what leads you to your conclusion.

Speech writing recipe

a) Summarise your view.

b) Give two reasons that lead you to this conclusion.

c) Explain why you reject each of the other two possibilities.

d) Recap your view and repeat your main reason.

In the Bible, St Paul says to a group of Christians: 'you are the body of Christ, and each one of you is a part of it.' This is a big idea that still inspires Christians today. What does it mean?

Starter → → → →

This is a poster that sometimes appears outside a church. What point is it making?

● People, not steeple

A church is a group of people, not a building. The word 'church' comes from a Greek word that means 'gathering'. The places where Christians meet are church buildings. Some churches gather in school halls or leisure centres. Some gather in grand cathedrals. Some gather in the open air under a palm tree or in a park or on a beach. Jesus called people to follow him. He never asked people to build special buildings all over the world, useful though they might be.

● The body of Christ

When St Paul said, 'you are the body of Christ, and each one of you is a part of it', he was writing to Christians in the city of Corinth. He had heard that they were arguing about how to follow Jesus and, just like today, they were splitting into different groups. He was telling them to forget their differences – they do not matter – all Christians are part of the body of Christ. Note that St Paul doesn't say that they are just *joined* to the body of Christ, he says that they *are* the body of Christ. Christians are Christ's hands, Christ's feet, Christ's body on earth and every part is important.

● One body – many parts

That fact that the Christian religion is split into many different traditions or denominations may not seem to fit in very well with this idea. Today in the UK, for example, you can find Anglican, Methodist, Catholic, Orthodox, Lutheran, Baptist and many more churches. A new style of assembly are the 'Community Churches' that usually meet in rented community buildings such as school halls and are often made up of Christians who have deliberately left the 'traditional' denominations. People's basic beliefs about God and Jesus are the same and most churches are friendly and support each other, but each type worships in different ways and believes different things about who should lead a church.

● WHAT WOULD ST PAUL THINK OF THIS?

This is just like the situation that St Paul was dealing with in Corinth when he told Christians there to forget their differences and to focus on the important thing – Jesus – that brings them together. But he also says there is nothing

▲ *In this medieval portrait of Jesus the artist shows the church being born out of the body of the dying Jesus*

1 What does the word 'church' mean?
2 Make a collage or a diagram to show the idea of the church being the body of Christ. For example, you could draw a simple outline of Jesus then cut and paste pictures of different Christians from around the world or different types of people.
3 Write a news report – 'An Unusual Birthday Party' – about Agnes' party, including quotes.

wrong with differences. Within the body of Christ he imagines a foot arguing with a hand: 'because I am not a hand I don't belong to the body' (1 Corinthians 12:14–20). This is obviously ridiculous – the body is not made up only of hands! So just as a healthy body has different parts with different functions, so it is with Christians. Christ's body has different parts, with different characters and different functions.

To Christians today, in all traditions, St Paul might well bring the same message – whichever denomination you belong to, you are all part of the body of Christ. Believe it and enjoy it!

● Diversity

Jesus called all sorts of people to follow him: rich, poor, clever, simple, and those who didn't quite fit into society at the time, such as lepers, tax collectors and women who had many lovers. His critics disapproved of his choice of friends but he welcomed them, whatever their past, and whatever their failings, as long as they genuinely wanted to follow him.

The same is true today. Jesus attracts many people with many different needs and backgrounds: healthy and sick, angry and forgiving, happy and sad. It is a rich mix but, in St Paul's words, 'all are part of the body of Christ' and so anyone who follows Jesus is welcome into the body of Christ. As part of that body, individual Christians learn to be more like Christ and to continue his mission on earth.

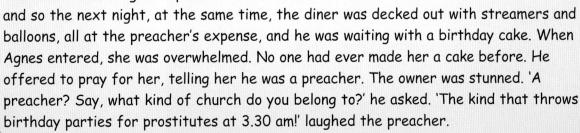

An Unusual Birthday Party

An American preacher was visiting Honolulu and, because of the time difference, he found himself looking for something to eat at 3.30 am. An old diner was open and he went in and ordered some food. As he was eating, a group of prostitutes came in, laughing and joking. One of them, Agnes, roared, 'It's my birthday tomorrow. I'm going to be 39!' Another mocked her, saying, 'What do you want me to do, bake you a cake?' Soon after, they left and went out on the streets again.

The preacher said that he felt the Holy Spirit prompt him to do something. He spoke to the owner of the diner and so the next night, at the same time, the diner was decked out with streamers and balloons, all at the preacher's expense, and he was waiting with a birthday cake. When Agnes entered, she was overwhelmed. No one had ever made her a cake before. He offered to pray for her, telling her he was a preacher. The owner was stunned. 'A preacher? Say, what kind of church do you belong to?' he asked. 'The kind that throws birthday parties for prostitutes at 3.30 am!' laughed the preacher.

Starter ➜ ➜ ➜

Describe a time when you shared a special meal with someone. It might have been a large gathering or a simple takeaway with some friends. What made it special?

4 List four different names that are used for the meal of bread and wine. You might be able to use your own research to find more than four.

5 Look at picture A.
a) How has the artist shown Jesus?
b) What is Jesus doing?
c) What is the relationship between Jesus and the disciples?

● Gathered in his name

Jesus said to his disciples, 'For where two or three come together in my name, I am there with them' (Matthew 18:20). In churches on Sundays there will be worship services with music, preaching and praying. During the week most churches will have social events such as children's groups and youth clubs, friendship clubs for the elderly, and charity events. There may be discussion groups, meeting in a church building or in people's homes. There may be counselling for people who need help with their marriage or their money. There may be teaching events, such as the Alpha Course, where the church tries to spread the message of Jesus to others. These are all part of what it means to be the Body of Christ and each event in its own way is a celebration of Jesus.

● Holy Communion

One feature of worship common to nearly all Christian churches is the sharing of bread and wine. They give it different names, such as Holy Communion, the Eucharist, the Lord's Supper or the Mass. Sharing food together is a sign of being a family, a team, a group of friends, but it's also important for other reasons.

● **THIS IS WHAT JESUS ASKED HIS DISCIPLES TO DO**

The night before he died, at the Last Supper, Jesus took bread and wine and gave it to his disciples. When he had shared these with them, he told them to carry on doing this whenever they met together. So whenever Christians share this special meal they are obeying Jesus and deepening their relationship with him.

● **IT BRINGS CHRIST AMONG THEM**

Jesus called himself the Bread of Life and also the True Vine. In those days bread was the most important food, and wine the most important drink. They were everyday things, not special, so he was comparing himself to the very things that everyone needed. But at the Eucharist these everyday things take on symbolic meaning. At the Last Supper Jesus said about the bread, 'This is my Body which is given for you' and about the wine, 'This is my Blood, given for you'. So every time Christians take the bread and wine it is a physical reminder of Jesus,

A

▲ The Last Supper, *painted by Emil Nolde, 1909*

I find great peace by praying before the Blessed Sacrament. It allows me to sit quietly in the presence of Jesus, just being near him. It is great radiotherapy for the soul!

that he is there among them and they are feeding on him.

Some Christians believe that when Jesus said 'This is my Body' and 'This is my Blood' he meant that the bread and wine literally become his body and blood. Roman Catholics call this **transubstantiation**, when the bread and wine still have the appearance of bread and wine but the underlying reality is Jesus, who is present with his people today. The bread that is reserved for this purpose is called the **Blessed Sacrament**. Sometimes a piece of this blessed bread is kept in a special cupboard called a **tabernacle** or in a decorative holder called a **monstrance**.

● IT IS A THANKSGIVING

Eucharist comes from a Greek word meaning 'thanksgiving'. The Eucharist is a thanksgiving for the death and resurrection of Jesus Christ. It may seem strange to give thanks for Jesus' death but, as you saw on page 34, Christians believe that his death was part of God's plan to save people. So, at Eucharist, Christians are giving thanks that Jesus died for their sakes and for their salvation.

❛ *Those who eat my flesh and drink my blood have eternal life, and I will raise them to life on the last day.* ❜

(John 6:54)

Sometimes when I am taking the bread and wine I feel that it is a time just for me and God – everyone else there at church just slips away – and I am there with my saviour and redeemer.

● Different customs

Different traditions take the meal in different ways. In Catholic or Orthodox churches you will find a lot of ritual and colourful robes. Some ring bells and offer up sweet-smelling incense. In most Protestant churches you will find it is much simpler. Some traditions allow children to take part, others don't. But, however it is celebrated, the words of Jesus are recalled from the Last Supper as the bread and wine are blessed.

Christians believe that the meal has extra importance because they are sharing it with hundreds of millions of other people in other countries. They may speak different languages, they may never meet, but they are all part of the same body.

6 Compare pictures B and C. Both show a Eucharist or Communion service but they are very different. Choose one and write a caption for it, explaining what you think it shows.

B

C

The Eucharist is not the only way to focus on Jesus. Here are some other symbols and rituals that Christians use.

Starter

Have you ever met anyone famous? Explain where it was, what happened, how you behaved and how you felt.

● **FOCUS ON … A GOSPEL**

For Christians, the Gospels are the centre of their faith, because Jesus is the centre of their faith. Some churches have a special procession when the Gospels are read. The Bible is held up high. Servers carry candles and incense. The candles remind people that Jesus is the Light of the World. The incense honours the presence of God in the words of Jesus. When the Gospel is read, the congregation stands – both to show respect and to show they are ready for action.

Some Bibles are printed with the words of Jesus in red so that they stand out clearly. These words of Jesus are read, prayed about, meditated upon and discussed with others. They are a guide through life and food for the soul of a believer.

● **FOCUS ON … A CRUCIFIX**

A crucifix is a small cross with a figure of Jesus upon it. Looking at the crucifix reminds believers of the love of God, of the God who became flesh and died for people. By looking at it, believers can feel sorrow for what Jesus had to go through, be sorry for their own sins or feel thankful to Jesus for their salvation.

Some churches have a particular ceremony on Good Friday that remembers the death of Jesus. A crucifix is held before the people and they come and pay their respects, by just looking at it, touching it, or kissing the wounds on the feet. It is a visual aid to recall the sufferings that Jesus once went through.

● **FOCUS ON … AN ICON**

Icons are painted images of Jesus or the saints. Icons are known as 'windows into heaven'. These can be kept at home, often in a special corner where the family says their prayers. In Orthodox churches these icons will be painted on a screen in front of the altar. Orthodox believers will cross themselves and kiss the icon before saying their prayers. Sometimes they will walk up to the icons and pray, right in the middle of a service, regardless of what the priest is doing.

The icons show the Glory of God, coming from the faces of Jesus or the saints. When believers look at an icon of Mary and the child Jesus, they are reminded that God took flesh through Mary. The icon is like a visual sermon.

● FOCUS ON ... THE SACRED HEART

Roman Catholics have a favourite image called the Sacred Heart of Jesus. In the seventeenth century a nun, St Mary Margaret, had a vision in which she saw the heart of Jesus ablaze with holy fire and surrounded by a crown of thorns. Jesus said to her, 'Here is the Heart who loved men so much.' The fire symbolises the love of God that lasts forever; the thorns are the suffering that Jesus went through. Many Catholics will have an image of the sacred heart in their homes.

● FOCUS ON ... A CANDLE

In Christianity candles are a symbol of the presence of God or Jesus. Many churches have a special Easter candle, called a Paschal candle, which has pins in it representing the five wounds of Christ. But the candle is mostly to celebrate the Resurrection and Jesus' victory over death. It is lit on the first service of Easter Sunday and is used throughout the year. For the Easter celebration people light their own smaller candles from it. Light suggests life and hope. Jesus is called the Light of the World.

● FOCUS ON ... A STORY

Some Christians read a story of Jesus healing someone or performing a miracle. Then they try to be still, breathing deeply, counting breaths, thinking of a peaceful scene. Next they imagine the scene in the Gospel story and start to relive this in their minds. They try to become one of the characters in the story. If the scene changes or unexpected people turn up, they allow this to happen and they follow its flow. This imaginative way of considering the Gospel stories can be very striking and personal. It is as if Jesus is speaking directly to the person meditating – giving them hope and direction.

1 a) Working with a partner, write five questions – some easy, some difficult – based on these two pages.

    b) Swap questions with another pair and then, without looking at this book, try to answer their questions.

2 Christians talk about having a relationship with Jesus. Choose one of the approaches described here and explain how it could deepen that relationship.

3 If you were a Christian wanting to feel closer to Jesus, which of these approaches would work best for you and why? Which would not work for you and why?

Some people find that their beliefs and their understanding of Jesus are strengthened by visiting places or seeing objects that are associated with him.

Think of a special place that you like to visit. It could be a sports ground, a graveside, a beauty spot, a mountain. Explain where it is and why it is special for you.

▲ The Star of Bethlehem in the Church of the Nativity

▲ A woman worships in the Church of the Holy Sepulchre

'I trembled with delight and with awe when I saw the burial place of Christ. It was as though peace fell on me and joy came up from within me … bubbling up. But I cried, too. For here my Lord had been laid out, dead, after suffering so terribly for me. This place speaks of death and resurrection, of the forgiveness of God.

▲ Eliseveta, a pilgrim from Russia

● The Church of the Nativity

The Church of the Nativity in Bethlehem claims to be built upon the site of Jesus' birth. A star is carved into the ground (see photo A) to mark what is thought to be the exact location of the manger. Worshippers travel here from all over the world and pray silently or bow down and kiss the area in devotion and thankfulness to God.

● The Holy Sepulchre

The tomb where Jesus was buried would have been remembered and visited by the early Christians. In the second century CE, the Emperor Hadrian had a pagan temple built on the site. Still, we have evidence of Christians visiting the site and paying their respects, such as a leading Christian called Mileto in CE 180. Much later, when the Emperor Constantine allowed Christians to worship freely within the Roman Empire, he sought to restore the ancient site as a place of pilgrimage in CE 326. His mother, Helena, had toured the Holy Land, checking on local traditions, and she believed that she had found the site of the tomb, known as the Holy Sepulchre. Constantine had a large church, called a basilica, built over this.

The basilica has been rebuilt several times. Now various Christian groups look after it. The key-holders to the tomb itself are members of two local Muslim families, the Judeh and the Nuseibeh. The Sepulchre is opened daily with a special ritual. A ladder is passed through a portal to one of the key-holders. He opens the lower lock on the door and then climbs the ladder to open the upper lock. Pilgrims enter the tomb area in silent awe. There they kneel and pray, touching the stone slab upon which they believe the body of Jesus once lay or resting their heads upon it. It is a holy moment and a sacred place.

▲ A stained-glass window at Walsingham showing Richeldis' vision

Walsingham

Walsingham in Norfolk has a shrine of the Virgin Mary. This was first built in 1061 when the lady of the manor, Richeldis de Faverches, claimed to have a vision of Mary and the child Jesus. The Virgin told her to build a replica of the house where Jesus was brought up in Nazareth. At the time, many people were making long and dangerous pilgrimages to the Holy Land where the Crusades would soon begin. This new house was to become a place of pilgrimage for all those who could not get to the east. In 1069 Augustinian friars took over care of 'England's Nazareth', as the shrine was called, and looked after it until it was destroyed in the sixteenth century CE by Henry VIII. Its proximity to the sea made it easy for ships to bring pilgrims from all over Europe. Pilgrims stopped first at the 'Slipper Chapel' and then walked the rest of the journey barefoot.

The shrine was rebuilt by an Anglican vicar, Fr Hope Patten, in 1931 and it has become a place of pilgrimage again. The old Slipper Chapel was reopened as the Roman Catholic shrine. The centre of the Shrine Church is the Holy House, built to Richeldis' original specifications and copying the dimensions of an ordinary family house in Nazareth. In the Holy House people light a candle to represent their prayer, for Jesus said he was the Light of the World. Along one wall are thanksgiving plaques placed by people whose prayers have been answered.

> I've travelled from north-east England to pray here and to ask for healing for my nephew who has very bad asthma. It is very peaceful in the Holy House and I've lit a candle for him.

▲ A pilgrim describing his visit to Walsingham

1 Look at pages 44–45. Which aspects of Christian belief do these places of pilgrimage focus on?
2 Some people find it feeds their faith to visit sacred places like these. Others find it doesn't help them at all to feel closer to Jesus. What reasons can you think of to explain these differences?
3 Design a poster to advertise one of these places of pilgrimage. What are you going to say to attract people to visit? Why should they think the place is special?

▲ Pilgrims pray in the silence of the Holy House in the Anglican shrine of Our Lady of Walsingham

● The Turin Shroud

This long strip of yellowing cloth is kept securely in the cathedral in Turin, Italy. It is known as the Holy Shroud. It bears the imprint of a crucified man.

The image on the cloth is like a photographic image. It is imprinted on the surface of the fibres. It is not made up of paint or any other substance. There is no trace of pigment or brush marks. It is a mystery how the image was made.

For centuries many people believed it to be the actual burial cloth of Jesus. The wounds are just right. There are also microscopic traces of plants on the cloth that come only from the Holy Land. As these people prayed before the shroud they believed that they were seeing the image of Jesus and that the image was caused by a burst of energy when the Resurrection happened.

Today there is great doubt: pieces of the cloth have been carbon dated, showing that it is only 700 or 800 years old. But some experts want to retest the cloth, arguing that the earlier samples were corrupted. The jury is still out.

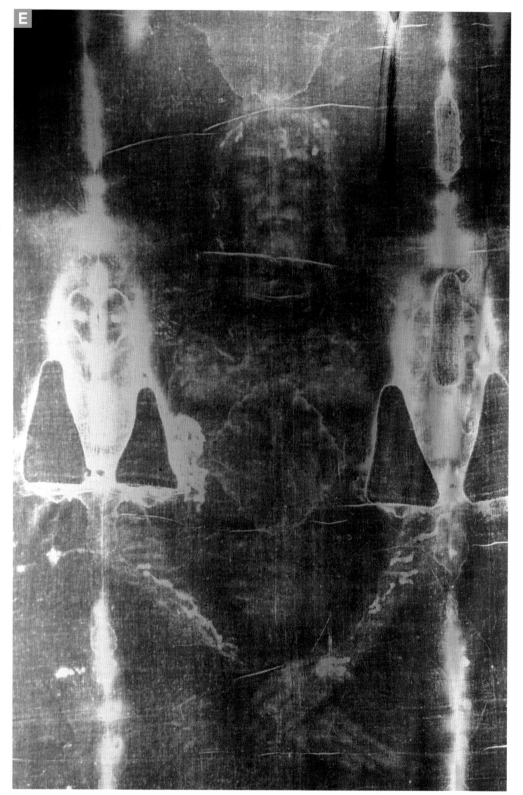

4 Work in pairs. One of you must argue that the Turin Shroud is the genuine burial cloth of Jesus, the other that it is not. Try to argue your case for at least a minute. Then swap roles and argue the opposite viewpoint.

5 'It doesn't matter if the shroud is real. All that matters is that it helps people to focus on Jesus.' Do you agree? Write two paragraphs summing up reasons for and against this statement, then state your own view.

Internet research

- Go to http://www.national gallery.org.uk/ then type 'Jesus' in the search box and you will find dozens of images from old paintings.
- Also try this website: http://www.religionfacts.com/jesus/image_gallery.html

Summary tasks

● Jesus arts exhibition

Create, on your own or with others, a Jesus arts exhibition. You could use pictures from this book or other items found from your own research. You could include paintings, stained glass or sculptures. You could add pictures you have made, for example, your collage from page 39. You could include music or songs. Images of Jesus are even found on T-shirts, flip-flops and surfboards.

You should include a written explanation of what you have chosen and why. Choose items that mean something to you or you have strong views about, as it will be easier to write about them.

Here are some ideas for presentation, but don't be limited by these. Do it your own way.

A BELIEF Choose a single belief, such as 'incarnation', and then choose images that show different aspects of this belief. Explain what each tells you about the belief.

A GALLERY Select five interesting items and write a record card like this about each one:

Title: _____
Artist: _____
Where I found it: _____
Content (what aspect of Jesus this focuses on): _____
Why I decided to include it: _____

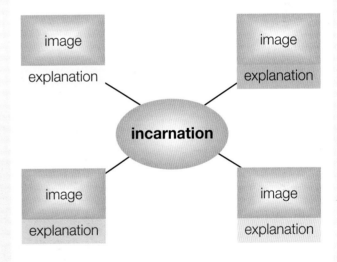

image
explanation

image
explanation

incarnation

image
explanation

image
explanation

ALL MY OWN WORK Through Sections 1 and 2 of this book you have been asked to create your own artwork. You could show this. For each piece, write your own evaluation: what aspect of Jesus it shows; why you chose to do it that way.

PAIRS Choose two strongly contrasting images, such as two representations of the crucifixion of Jesus. Display them side by side and explain how they differ in their interpretation. Explain what aspect of the crucifixion they focus on. Explain which one you most like and why.

● Discuss

Over the past few weeks you have studied many different images of Jesus. Think about then discuss how and why it helps believers to express their beliefs and ideas in the creative arts.

- Is artwork more powerful than words?
- Are there ideas that only art or music can convey?
- Why do some believers want churches that are full of images, such as the church on page 31, while others dislike them and find the images a distraction?

47

UNIT 3.1 | Jesus' values

Christians believe that if they want to live right they should act, think and live like Jesus. He is their role model. But people today don't always face the same situations as Jesus, so Christians must look behind Jesus' words and actions to find his values.

Starter

Who is your role model? Whom do you most want to be like? Explain why you chose that person and explain how they have influenced what you do or how you dress or speak.

1 Pages 48–50 give examples of Jesus' words, stories and actions as recorded in the Gospels. Using these, or others that you know, make a concept map of Jesus' values. You could start like this.

Jesus' values
forgiveness
love
even for enemies

Love your enemies and pray for those who persecute you so that you may become the children of your Father in heaven (Matthew 5:44–45)

Do not judge others, so that God will not judge you, for God will judge you in the same way as you judge others and he will apply to you the same rules you apply to others (Matthew 7:1–2)

If anyone slaps you on the right cheek, let him slap your left cheek too (Matthew 5:39)

● **THE UNFORGIVING SERVANT** (Matthew 18:21–35)

A servant owed a king a great deal of money but could not pay. The king let him off. But then the forgiven servant saw a neighbour in the street who owed him a tiny amount of money. He had the neighbour arrested for not paying his debt. The king was angry. He put the servant in prison. He had forgiven him so much and yet the servant would not forgive a little!

● **THE WOMAN AT THE WELL** (John 4:5–30)

One day, in Samaria, Jesus sat by a well. A woman came to collect water. Normally a Jew would not talk to a Samaritan. Even less would a rabbi talk to a woman he didn't know, especially one like this who had been married four times and was now living with a man who was not her husband. But Jesus ignored these rules. He talked to her for a long time about her life and how he could offer her springs of living water that could bubble up within her. He did not condone her sin, but he showed mercy and compassion.

● **THE WOMAN WITH AN ISSUE OF BLOOD** (Mark 5:25–34)

A woman pushed her way through a crowd to touch Jesus' robe. She thought that if only she could reach out to him in this way, she might be healed. For years she had had a problem with a flow of blood that no doctor had been able to cure. Jesus knew immediately that power had gone out from him and he asked who had touched him. He blessed her and declared her healed.

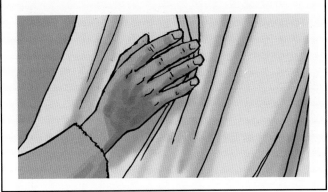

● **THE POOR WIDOW** (Luke 21:1–4)

Jesus spoke often about wealth. He once praised a widow for putting a small coin in the Temple collection, saying that she had given more (from her heart) than a rich man who put in a few more coins in passing. By this, he meant that God looks at the heart and so at people's motives. In the Sermon on the Mount, Jesus says, 'Blessed are the poor, for theirs is the kingdom of God.' He told people to forgive their debtors.

● **OVERTURNING THE TABLES IN THE TEMPLE**

(Luke 19:45–46)

Jesus had gone to the Temple to pray, but all around it were traders and money-changers. He overturned their tables, shouting that they had turned a house of prayer into a den of thieves.

▲ Christ expels the money-changers from the Temple, *painted by Edward Burra*

● **MARY AND MARTHA**
(Luke 10:38–42)

Mary and Martha were sisters who looked after Jesus and the disciples. Martha was busy preparing food when Jesus was trying to teach them about the kingdom of God. Mary sat at his feet to listen but Martha fretted. He scolded Martha but praised Mary.

● **WASHING THE DISCIPLES' FEET** (John 13:1–20)

At the Last Supper before he died, Jesus laid aside his cloak and washed his disciples' feet.

▲ Jesus Washing Peter's Feet, *painted by Ford Madox Brown, 1876*

2 Why do you think the disciples were surprised that Jesus spoke to the woman at the well (page 49)? What did she tell other people about him?
3 Why was Mary praised and Martha scolded by Jesus? Is this fair?
4 Look at the following newspaper headlines. Which do you think would have made Jesus most angry?
  a) Traffic jam clogs the M6
  b) Children as young as 10 recruited by drug gangs
  c) Terrorists blow up Twin Towers
  d) Football fans fined for racist chanting
  e) The hottest summer on record – yet again!
  f) Thousands imprisoned for speaking out against government
  g) Famine and war in Darfur
  h) Cathedral starts to charge entry fee to visitors

➜ ➜ ➜ ➜   Coming up

At the end of Section 3 you will be giving an LLJ award to one of the people featured there. A 'Lives Like Jesus' award should be given to the person who has been the most successful in living their life according to the values of Jesus. To start you thinking about this, choose the three most important values from your concept map. ➜

Serving others is an important part of being like Jesus. Here are two case studies of modern people who have given their lives to serving others.

Starter

Describe an occasion when you helped someone. Why did you do it? What was the result?

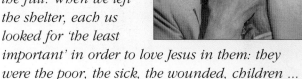

● Chiara Lubich: Focolare

I was twenty-three years old and my friends were the same age or younger. We were in Trento, where we were born, and the war was destroying everything. Each of us had a dream. One wanted to have a family and was waiting for her fiancé to return from the front. Another was busy decorating her house which she loved. I believed that I could find fulfilment by studying philosophy ...

But ... the fiancé never returned; that house collapsed; I could not travel to the university because of the war.

What could we do? Was there an ideal that no bomb could destroy, for which it was worth spending our life? At once, the light came: yes there was. It was God. God who in those moments of war and hatred, revealed Himself to us for what He truly is: Love. It all happened in an instant. We decided to make God the reason for our lives.

But how? We wanted to do as Jesus did, to do the Father's will and not our own. Indeed, we wanted to be another little Jesus. We must all do our part. We wanted to do it.

The war was ruthless. Many times, day and night, we had to go to the air-raid shelter. When the sirens sounded, we had to run and could take nothing with us except one small book: the Gospel. It was in the Gospel that we found out how to do God's will, how to be another Jesus. We opened the Gospel and read it: **'Whatever you did for one of the least important of these members of my family, you did it for me'** *(Matthew 25:40).*

Those words which we had read so many times before, now seemed very new to us, as if a light were illuminating them one by one from underneath. We felt urged to live them to the full. When we left the shelter, each us looked for 'the least important' in order to love Jesus in them: they were the poor, the sick, the wounded, children ...

We looked for them in the streets, to write down their names and addresses in order to reach and help them. We invited them to our dinner table, giving them the best seats.

Although we ourselves had very little, nothing was lacking because the Gospel says: **'Give to others, and God will give to you'** *(Luke 6:38). We gave the little we had and many things came back, so many that sacks and packages filled the corridor of our house every day.*

The Gospel tells us: **'Ask, and you will receive'** *(Luke 11:9). So, one day in church, we asked. 'I need a pair of shoes, size 42, for you (in that poor man)', and, coming out of the church, a woman handed us a pair of shoes, size 42.*

The Gospel says, **'Be concerned above everything else with the kingdom of God ... and he will provide you with all ... things'** *(Matthew 6:33). We tried to let Jesus reign in us by living His Word, and we received everything, all that we needed. We were happy. Everything promised in the Gospel came true. We felt that we were living a miracle. We always knew that the Gospel was true. But then we saw it for ourselves.*

(Adapted from http://www.focolare.org)

▶ *Bukas Palad, a Focolare social project in a shanty town near Manila in the Philippines*

1 What did Chiara mean when she asked God for a pair of shoes 'for you (in that poor man)'?

2 Some of the sayings of Jesus that inspired the first members of Focolare are highlighted. Choose one and write a paragraph explaining what this meant to them and how they applied it.

Web check

3 Compare these two websites: http://www.focolare.org http://www.focolare.net

a) Which is the official one? How do you know?

b) How do they differ in their opinion of Focolare?

Focolare means 'hearth' or 'fireplace'. People who were helped by Chiara and her friends sensed so much love from them that they gave them this nickname and it stuck. Fifty years later, Focolare has become a worldwide movement with thousands of members of all ages, backgrounds, vocations and cultures. Originally, members were Catholics but this expanded to include not only other Christians but also people of other faiths and even those with no particular faith. Some members live in dedicated small communities called Focolare Centres; others live in wider society. All members believe in the spirituality of the movement and the sense of experiencing God together. It is not so much about studying scripture, more about putting it into practice. The focus is on unity, after the Bible verse that inspired Chiara, 'May they all be one' (John 17:21).

It is not a specifically a charity, although many members, like other religious people, are involved in charitable works. One group in Rome, for example, goes out on the streets ministering to the homeless. Food and hot drinks are given out. One young woman went frequently to speak to an old woman huddled in a doorway. She took off the woman's socks and bathed her sore and swollen feet, then put on fresh socks and blessed her.

The Focolare movement has been recognised by religious leaders as a positive force. In 1964, Pope Paul VI called it a 'work of God'. In 1984, Pope John Paul II visited the movement's headquarters and spoke of the 'radicalism of love' that characterises the gifts of the Holy Spirit. The movement, which focuses on the Gospels and the life of Mary, has its roots in Catholicism. However, Chiara Lubich has met with many other Christian leaders, who have spoken of their desire for unity, as well as with members of other faiths.

Heather Reynolds: God's Golden Acre

▶ *Heather Reynolds with orphaned children*

Web check

4 God's Golden Acre has a website in the UK: http://www.gods goldenacre.org.uk/ This website makes no mention of Heather Reynolds' Christian beliefs or her spiritual motivation. Why do you think that might be?

5 'The greatest good comes out of the greatest suffering.' Explain what this means with reference to Chiara Lubich or Heather Reynolds.

6 List the ways in which Chiara Lubich or Heather Reynolds has followed the example of Jesus (e.g. 'by helping the poorest people').

7 Do you think that either Chiara Lubich or Heather Reynolds sets an example that you would like to follow in your own life? Explain with reasons.

Heather Reynolds became a Christian as a young woman. She took her faith seriously. She wanted to serve God better and she prayed to God to be given a calling.

Some years later, in 1993, she was travelling in Uganda. She stopped to get some water from a spring and saw a group of children. She spoke to them and found out they were orphans whose parents had died of AIDS. They were trying to look after themselves and each other as best they could but it was hard. She went with the children to where they lived. As she knelt beside a dying child in a hut, she knew what she had to do with her life. She pledged to give herself to such children. This was her calling. She prayed, 'God, from this day on I will help every child in need, every child that needs a home, every child that crosses my path.'

Later, she and her sculptor husband, Patrick, started to take children into their home in KwaZulu-Natal. They established a community that cares for nearly 100 orphans. They call this place 'God's Golden Acre'. Many orphans are healthy, but those infected with HIV are unlikely to live past their fourth birthday, so the task is to help them die with dignity in loving surroundings.

A team of nurses and helpers now help Heather. The locals know her as 'mawethu', Zulu for 'our mother'. A nurse helping her has described her this way: 'She is the personification, in our era, of the Good Samaritan.'

Heather and Patrick donated all their savings to their project and then 'lived by faith', which means depending on God to provide what they need. They followed the example of Jesus who gave up all he had to follow his mission and called on his followers to do the same. He told his disciples not to worry about clothes and food and that God would provide (Matthew 6:24–34). Heather and Patrick say they have seen many miracles of God's provision.

Jesus taught a lot about money. In fact he has more to say about money than some supposedly religious topics such as heaven and hell. He himself lived in poverty. Is that what he expects of all his followers?

1 Which of the following statements best summarises the point of the story of the rich young man?

● Everyone should be poor like Jesus

● Everyone who wants to follow Jesus should be poor like him

● If money is your main object in life, you must give it away if you want to follow Jesus

● It doesn't matter how rich you are as long as you use money well.

● What did Jesus say or do?

● THE RICH YOUNG MAN

Jesus spoke to many people and cured plenty but he called very few to follow him in a special way. Besides the twelve disciples, the Gospels mention one young man. He asked Jesus a question about finding eternal life. Jesus told him that he had done much to seek God but there was one more thing he must do. He must sell all that he had and follow Jesus. The young man went away, sad and deeply troubled, for he was rich. Jesus felt sad too, and the Bible says that he felt only love for the man. Jesus turned to his disciples and said, 'Children, how hard it is for those who trust in riches to enter the kingdom of God! It is easier for a camel to go through the eye of a needle than for a rich man to enter the kingdom of God.'

This may seem funny today but it probably meant something more down to earth then. Jesus might have been referring to a gate in Jerusalem known as 'the needle's eye', which a heavily laden camel would not have been able to pass through unless it shed its burdens. Likewise, if people are distracted by wealth and lust for money, they cannot follow Jesus as a disciple.

● OTHER EXAMPLES

Did Jesus reject all wealth? Does he want all Christians to live by faith and to 'drop out'? His close disciples, the twelve, felt called to do so but the story of the young man is the only example of Jesus counselling someone in this way. He helped and spoke to many other people but he didn't make such a demand of them. See what Zacchaeus did (Luke 19:1–10). Although some Christians today might feel the call to sell all their possessions and to live by faith, many other Christians say their calling is to earn money and to use it wisely.

2 Look up the story of King Midas. Write a modern version in a Christian context.

3 Discuss with a partner:
a) What is similar about St Francis and Laurie Beth Jones?
b) What is different?
c) Could they both be right?

4 List the ways in which the people featured on these two pages have followed the example of Jesus (e.g. 'Laurie Beth Jones has learned from Jesus' sense of mission').

Web check

5 Laurie Beth Jones has her own website: https://www.lauriebethjones.com. What can you find out about her beliefs from this site?

● How have Christians responded?

● **ST FRANCIS OF ASSISI**

Francis Bernardone was the son of a wealthy cloth merchant in Assisi, Italy. He was taken prisoner while fighting in a war and became very ill. When he came home, he thought again about his life. He read the Gospels and decided to live simply. He prayed in the ruins of the old church of San Damiano. He felt God telling him to rebuild the church. At first, he took this literally, so he rebuilt San Damiano with the help of close friends. Later, he realised that his call was bigger, that God wanted him to help renew the Church as a whole. In 1209–10 he gained permission from the Pope to found a new order of friars, of wandering preachers.

Just as his work was starting, his father met him in the town square and demanded that he return home and give up such nonsense. His father wanted him to help run the family business. There, in front of his father and to the shock of everyone around him, Francis stripped off all his clothes and handed them to his father, saying, 'Now I owe you nothing.' From then on Francis wore a simple robe and shaved his head as a monk. He had given up everything he owned.

His life's work was very successful. Thousands joined the order he founded – the Franciscans – and lived by the vows of poverty, chastity and obedience.

▲ St Francis Renounces his Father's Goods and Earthly Wealth, *wall painting by Giotto di Bondone, 1297–99*

● **LAURIE BETH JONES**

Laurie Beth Jones (right) is an American best-selling author and speaker who has built her reputation around a book called *Jesus CEO*. This takes the methods and example of Jesus and shows how business leaders and ordinary people can learn from them to make their lives more successful. She teaches 'the Path' to finding out who you are and where God will guide you, so that you can be successful in life in whatever you do:

❝*A clearly defined mission will serve you as a compass and a sword by keeping you moving in the right direction and cutting away distractions. People who craft carefully defined missions have always led and surpassed those who have none. Are you travelling your path or someone else's?*❞

She also has a special programme for teaching young people how to learn the secrets of success. She herself has had a successful life and enjoys the fruits of that success – she is wealthy and popular. She is able to commute between her foundation's headquarters in Arizona and her horse ranch in Texas.

Our modern world is a violent place. Historians suggest that there are more wars going on now than at any time in history. War between countries is seen as an acceptable way of solving problems. Gun crime and teenage victims often make the news headlines. But behind these headlines are desperate stories of suffering and sadness – people whose lives are ripped apart by war or crime. What is the Christian response to such a situation? How can Christians follow a way of peace in a violent world?

Starter → → → →

Look carefully at picture A and discuss it with a partner. What is going on? What do you make of it? Who do you think might have made a picture like this and why?

● **What did Jesus say and do?**

Picture B shows the arrest of Jesus. As the soldiers came to take Jesus away, Peter in his anger took up a sword. He swung it at a servant of the High Priest, Malchus, and sliced off his ear. Jesus stopped Peter and said, 'Put your sword away! Shall I not drink the cup the Father has given me?'

It was a critical moment. The disciples were waiting and wondering if Jesus would strike down the guards and give them a signal to fight. But Jesus gave himself up, believing that it was God's plan for him to die on the cross as a sacrifice for the sins of the world. Jesus embraced the way of peace and not violence.

Several times in his teaching, Jesus urged people to be peacemakers and to avoid violence, such as: 'Happy are those who work for peace; God will call them his children!' (Matthew 5:9). It is one of his clearest messages. Remember that this was at a time when many of his fellow Jews wanted to fight the Romans who were occupying their land. Indeed some thought that that was what the Messiah was supposed to do – to lead an armed uprising against the Romans.

◀ The Betrayal, *engraved by Albrecht Dürer, 1508*

How have Christians responded?

1 Read John 18:1–11 and look at picture B. Write a diary entry for Peter later that day. What might he have felt?
2 Discuss in groups whether you think it is ever right to fight in a war. Give reasons that might make you decide for or against. You could look at picture I on page 31.
3 How was the behaviour of St Francis of Assisi daring and different?

JUST WAR?

Christians have not always avoided violence. Some believe that there are times when fighting a war must happen to right a wrong. If the result of not fighting sees many innocent people hurt and mistreated, such as happened to the Jews in World War II, is it fair to stand back and let it happen? The Churches have worked out ideas of a 'just war' to deal with such situations. To declare a war 'just', there are strict conditions such as avoiding any hurt to civilians as far as possible and needing to right a wrong.

ST FRANCIS THE PEACEMAKER

The Crusades were a series of campaigns fought in the Holy Land in the Middle Ages to free Christian sites from Muslim control. Many saw this as a just cause then (whatever we might think now) and entered the battles with a great sense of duty. However, others were bloodthirsty and out for what they could get. Terrible things were done by men wearing the Christian cross on their uniforms. A Christian might argue that war is a failure of the human heart, when all attempts to make peace break down.

St Francis of Assisi lived at this time. He was appalled by the behaviour of the Crusaders. He came to believe that only peaceful persuasion and living a holy life would make the Saracen Muslims think differently about the Christian faith. He backed up his words with brave actions. At great risk to his own life, he travelled in peace to see the Sultan in Egypt. The Sultan honoured him as a holy man. Today St Francis is the patron saint of peacemakers.

▼ *Scene from a Crusader battle from the film* Kingdom of Heaven

C

● David Wilkerson: bringing peace to gangland

In 1958 David Wilkerson, a young minister from Philipsburg, USA, saw a news item about teenage boys in New York who had been arrested for murder. They belonged to a street gang called the Dragons. As they terrorised parts of the city, a 15-year-old polio victim, Michael Farmer, had been killed. David felt a call from God to go to these youths and preach God's love to them. He felt God's pain for them as they were lost, out on the streets, abusing drugs and probably from difficult homes.

He found his way to New York. He was photographed trying to get into the courtroom and holding up his Bible. Because of this he met the gangs. They thought he was on their side and they started to listen. But some members were tough and threatened him. The hardest was Nicky Cruz, a boy who had been beaten and sent away from home as a young child. He had made his way on the streets, fighting hard. Nicky slapped David across the face and told him to go to hell. He held up a flick-knife to threaten him. David responded by saying that even if Nicky cut him into a thousand pieces, every one of these would still love him. Nicky backed off and ran. He hated the preacher and hated to hear about love.

NICKY CRUZ
WITH JAMIE BUCKINGHAM
Run Baby Run

'You could cut me in a thousand pieces and lay them out on the street. But every piece would cry out, Jesus loves you. And you'll never be able to run from that.'

OVER TWELVE MILLION COPIES SOLD

Eventually, David and some local Christians held a mission. They rented a theatre and David preached to the assembled gangs. Violence could have erupted at any minute. Nicky, in fact, had planned to steal the offering that was taken. Yet, as David spoke, Nicky was overwhelmed. He had felt pursued by God for weeks, troubled in his conscience, and he broke down in tears. He and several others knelt down on the stage and made a commitment to follow Jesus. This was just the start for them, and David realised that they needed special help to clean up their lives. He established Teen Challenge centres where they and others could stay to come off drugs, seek counsel and pray.

Nicky Cruz became a minister himself. He still tours the world telling his story, which he also described in his book *Run Baby Run* (left). David wrote his version in *The Cross and the Switchblade.*

4 Why do you think people join gangs?
5 What do you think happened in the gang after Nicky Cruz left?
6 What do you think might happen to David Wilkerson or Nicky Cruz if he came to work among gangs in Britain today?

● Dietrich Bonhoeffer's choice

▶ *Dietrich Bonhoeffer in London, 1939*

7 Bonhoeffer compared his situation to having a gun in your hand and seeing a madman driving a car down the road, aimed straight at a child on the pavement. If you were in that situation and could use the gun to save the child, what would you do? What are your options? Which would you choose?

8 Imagine you are Bonhoeffer. Write a letter to a pacifist friend explaining why you got involved in the plot to kill Hitler.

Dietrich Bonhoeffer was a 27-year-old Lutheran pastor in Berlin when Hitler and the Nazis became leaders of Germany in 1933. He was shocked by Hitler's rise to power and deeply disturbed by Hitler's hatred of the Jews. He tried to get his fellow ministers in Berlin to go on strike, for example by refusing to take funerals, unless the Nazis toned down their policies. He quoted from the Bible: 'Speak up for people who cannot speak for themselves. Protect the rights of all who are helpless' (Proverbs 31:8). The strike failed but when Hitler set up a new Reich (state) church, whose ministers had to swear an oath of loyalty to Hitler, Bonhoeffer helped to set up the Confessing Church, whose ministers refused to take this oath. Their loyalty was to Christ.

The Confessing Church was declared illegal but from 1935 to 1937 Bonhoeffer trained its ministers at Finkenwalde, where the trainees lived as a community. When the Nazi secret police – the Gestapo – closed this down, the trainees continued to meet in a country house until this too was closed in 1940. During this period, Bonhoeffer wrote his famous book, *The Cost of Discipleship*, which challenged Christians to take risks for God and to speak up for truth. He also set up a secret organisation to get Jews out of Germany to safety.

Eventually, Bonhoeffer became convinced that these measures were not enough. Hitler had to be killed. He was a madman who was causing immense suffering. Bonhoeffer and his brother-in-law joined a plot to assassinate Hitler. The plot failed, and in 1943 Bonhoeffer was arrested with several others and held in Tegel prison in Berlin. When a second attempt failed in 1944, he was transferred to Flossenburg concentration camp. On 9 April 1945 he was taken into woods and hanged with other prisoners. He showed great courage. He was seen praying fervently before being led out to his death. This moved one of his guards who later said: 'The devotion and evident conviction of being heard, that I saw in the prayer of this intensely captivating man, moved me to the depths.'

Bonhoeffer had always been a pacifist (opposed to all war). He followed the teachings of Jesus about non-violence and praying for your enemies. He knew the risks of what he did and the wisdom of Jesus' words, 'All who take the sword will die by the sword' (Matthew 26:52). But he decided that killing Hitler, while wrong, was a 'greater good' because so many innocent lives might be saved that way.

● The Community of the Cross of Nails

On 14 November 1940, German bombers left France en route to Coventry. The night was clear and soon the bombs started falling on the city. The bombers' targets were the factories of Coventry but the people and their homes were also hit in the process. Soon vast areas of the city were ablaze. By 8 o'clock, the first bombs struck the old cathedral. It was soon a seething mass of flames. By early morning its roof had gone and the whole cathedral lay open to the sky.

The military response to the bombing of Coventry and other British cities was huge. In 1941 the RAF launched massive raids on Germany. In 1945, with the war effectively won, the city of Dresden was hit in one of the worst attacks of the whole war. Over 25,000 people were killed and, just like Coventry, their cathedral was destroyed.

In Coventry – among the people who suffered – there was a different spirit. After the raid, the cathedral's stonemason found two pieces of wood which had fallen in the shape of a cross. It was like a promise to him. It was as if the cathedral had been 'crucified' but, just like Jesus, would rise again.

A local vicar used nails from the roof beams and formed them into a symbolic cross like this (picture D). Many more crosses of nails were made and distributed. The aim was to rebuild the people and places destroyed by violence and to reconcile them – help them to forgive each other and make peace. The Community of the Cross of Nails was set up, and today it is a worldwide network of over 170 organisations, united by this symbol, who work for peace where they live.

In the 1960s a new cathedral was built. The ruins of the old Coventry Cathedral were preserved next to it. Inside these ruins the old altar was left, with its cross of charred wood, and in front is the simple cross of nails. Soon after the war the community helped rebuild a hospital wing in Dresden, which had been destroyed by British bombers. Later they built a house of reconciliation in Northern Ireland when the community was being torn apart by terrorist violence. They also created an international centre for reconciliation which is still working in places such as Israel/Palestine. Copies of the cross of nails are used at special services around the world as a symbol of the evil that human beings can do, and of the power of love and forgiveness.

D
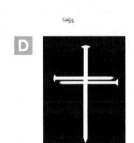

▲ The symbol of the Community of the Cross of Nails

E

▲ The replica charred cross and altar in Coventry Cathedral. A special reconciliation prayer is said here each Friday at 12.00 noon. Part of this prayer says, 'Be kind to one another, tender hearted, forgiving one another, as God in Christ forgave you'

9 Using your own words, write a one-sentence definition of the term 'reconciliation'.

10 As a class or in groups, suggest places or situations around the world which you think need reconciliation.

11 Choose one of those places and find two pictures from the internet or from newspapers or magazines to show or symbolise the people who are against each other or at war with each other. Paste the images side by side and write a reconciliation prayer beneath. It doesn't need to be a religious prayer.

12 List the ways in which the people featured on these pages have followed the example of Jesus (e.g. 'by forgiving those who bombed Coventry').

13 Do you think it is:
a) always right **b)** sometimes right **c)** always wrong
for a Christian to resist evil by force? Give your reasons.

Summary tasks

● The 'Live Like Jesus' award

A new award has been created. The LLJ award is for any individual or organisation that Lives Like Jesus. Each of the people in this section is nominated and, if you wish, you can nominate any other people who you think deserve an award.

1 Fill out a chart like this to summarise what each person has done to follow the example of Jesus:

Person	Place	What they did	Which values of Jesus they were living by	Comment

2 Choose one person who you think most deserves the award and write a short speech to be given at the award ceremony. Your speech should refer to some of the values that you recorded in your concept map of Jesus' values (page 48).

3 Make your speech to the class.

● The Jesus jigsaw

Through this book you have studied various aspects of Jesus' life and Christian beliefs about him. What do you think of him now? This final activity is to help you explore and express your ideas about Jesus.

You will need a copy of these jigsaw pieces. You can download your own version from www.hoddersamplepages.co.uk

Draw or write on each piece some aspect of Jesus that has stuck in your mind or challenged you or confused you. For example:

● compassion for the poor
● cry for justice
● servant of God
● God made man
● mystery.

Cut out the pieces and complete the jigsaw. Paste it on to paper or card. Then write an explanation of your completed jigsaw.

Index